T0352622

HEAR ME NOW!

I have made my "best faith effort" to ensure that everything in the text and videos is vegan (free of animal products or animal exploitation). However, we can all make mistakes. Just because anything is shown in this book or videos does not ensure that it is vegan. A product shown may also become "not vegan" in the future. You must still do your due diligence when you purchase products to guarantee they are vegan. This book or videos do not abdicate your responsibility of checking things for yourself. Always check for yourself with anything in life.

I have tried to ensure that the information here is accurate, but disclaim all liability in connection with the use of this book.

This book is in no way intended to replace, countermand, or conflict with the advice given to you by your own physician.

For a list of gluten free substitutions for the recipes in this book, go to:
http://veganblackmetalchef.com/seitanic-spellbook-gluten-free/ or scan this QR code:

ISBN 978-1-57067-385-6

Printed in China
Book Publishing Company / PO Box 99 / Summertown, TN 38483 / 888-260-8458 / bookpubco.com
Printed with vegan ink on responsibly harvested paper stock certified by the Forest Stewardship Council. us.fsc.org

THE SEITANIC SPELLBOOK

RECIPES AND RANTINGS OF THE
VEGAN BLACK METAL CHEF

THANK YOU

The production of this book was crowd-funded. It was only brought into physical existence because you the core fans, willed it. For this, I am eternally grateful and cannot thank you enough.

The goal to get this book printed felt near-unreachable in the beginning. It is only due to your awesome support that these thoughts and insecurities were crushed within the first week.

I will not stop showing the world how good, easy, cheap, and wise the vegan path is, for as long as I live Until every cage is empty.

It is my sincerest hope that you get serious usefulness out of the methods and information contained within.

Special thanks to three backers in particular that went above and beyond. Every amount contributed much to the making of this book, but three people made incredibly generous donations that go far beyond an even exchange of value:

Lynn Frier, Malila N. Robinson, and Judith Manowitz.

Another special thanks to Susan Rudin for her generous giving of time and help with the book.

And last but not least the team at the publishing house Éditions l'Âge Homme.

THANK YOU!

Table of Contents

HISPANIC & LATINO ORACLE OF INSPIRATION

INDIAN ORACLE OF INSPIRATION

ITALIAN ORACLE OF INSPIRATION

MIDDLE EASTERN ORACLE OF INSPIRATION

VEGAN MEAT ORACLE OF INSPIRATION

In the Beginning

It's time for a culinary enema…bend your mind over.

It's time to learn how to cook serious vegan food, of utmost quality, quickly and cheaply in the real world.

This book does not care about tradition.

Let's talk about tradition for just one moment. If you are going to flip out about culinary tradition, this cookbook is not for you. I am teaching you how to make food, the way I make it. I claim to make awesome food. If you don't believe me, just ask everyone who has had my food. They all think it's fucking great. Not only will this book teach you how to make mind blowing food, but it will teach you the basic concepts for you to make your own incredible shit any way you like. You will be able to take a giant pile of whatever the fuck is in the house and know how to make magic.

Not to say that traditional food or cooking is bad. I'm sure many of the cooking concepts in here are part of many ancient traditions. Nothing new under the sun. I am just making clear that I pay no special regard to it when it gets in the way of making food mortals shall kill for.

RICE

The one thing to go crazy with and really expand upon in your life, is to try out different types of rice. There is a tremendous variety of rice, and I am not saying to get all of them. However, tailoring a few types of rice with the types of food you are eating, will enhance the experience and flavor three-fold. The wrong rice can ruin a dish. The perfect rice can carry a dish.

Throughout each section there will be a sidebar titled "Rice of the Realm." Read these and heed their call.

The second thing to know about this book is that I cheat all over the place. Yes, I use prepared spices/spice blends, and any shortcut I can show you that abides by the principles of: 1) It tastes awesome. 2) It's totally not worth your time to make this shit from scratch.

We live in the real world. The real world has all sorts of luxuries of our global civilization. Hell, if you really wanted to make food from scratch, you would grow your own wheat or whatever from seeds, mill that shit when it's ready on your millstone, collect huge metal tubs of salt water to evaporate, or mine your own salt, etc. Come on, you are a REAL cook, aren't you?

I shall also divulge cooking tips and everything I have found useful in the world of personal development and mysticism. What you feed your mind is equally important as what you feed your body.

May you actually use and get use from this book.

EURO
AMERICAN

Introduction – EuroAmerican

The Euro-American cultures are a warlike breed. This is because the food itself in these cultures wants to kill you!

While neither the dishes here, nor anywhere in this book, are particularly "low calorie," they might kill you less fast than their animal-derived counterparts. If you want to see fruit or salad in this book, peer into the Oracle of Inspiration on page 45. Where you will be told to eat some fucking fruit, or a god-damned salad. That goes without saying, but I said it.

The meals in this section and throughout this book are hearty, filling meals, dispelling the puny myth that "vegan food does not fill you up" or "leaves you hungry." People shall literally eat their words upon the application of this text.

I shall begin with a universal main concept: more shit (ingredients or steps) often makes things worse, not better. Make everything only as complex as it needs to be. Every meal does not have to have every ingredient in it. Think about this as you make each and every item in this book.

I WOULD BE VEGAN EVEN IF IT WAS LESS HEALTHY FOR YOU

The overall health benefits that veganism often brings are a great icing on the cake. However, I would be vegan even if it was less healthy for you. Veganism is about compassion, leaving animals largely alone, and an incredible exploration of plant-based foods, among other things. I take no supplements, but even if I had to, I would choose that over the exploitation of animals. One thing about health is certain: the standard American diet is killing us, putting countless creatures through constant hell, and bankrupting our world through costly preventable illnesses. Veganism just happens to be a big piece of the answer, but even if it was not, I would still choose it.

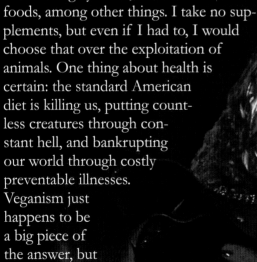

GRAVIES

Gravies in Black

SPELL REAGENTS
(INGREDIENTS)

VEGETABLE BROTH
- **Flour** *(I use self-rising flour since I use it everywhere else)*
- **Vegan butter**
- **Soy sauce** *(to make them dark)* **or salt** *(to keep them light)*
- **Pepper**
- **Italian seasoning** *(optional)*

FOR SAUSAGE GRAVY
- **Seitan or other vegan meat**
- **High-fat coconut milk** *(see the Thai curry recipe on page 74 for info on the coconut milk)*

FOR ROASTED GARLIC GRAVY
- **Roasted garlic**

FOR MUSHROOM GRAVY
- **Mushrooms** *(button, crimini, or portobello)*

Gravy is broth and fat! Let this principle ring true to your ears and tongue. Here we shall call upon three great gravies that escort us till our final rest. The key similarity to all of them is broth, fat, soy sauce or salt, pepper, and flour for thickening.

Let us divine the secrets one by one. CONTINUED

MUSHROOM GRAVY

The easiest of all the gravy rituals, requiring no preparation.

1. Heat some vegan butter in a pan. It shall appear as a golden nectar of the gods. Sauté finely-chopped mushrooms upon the divine butter. Summon a small amount of flour and sauté until brown.

2. Pour a deluge of vegetable broth into this crucible. It shall thicken up to perfection. Add a small amount of soy sauce and simmer for a few minutes.

   If too flavorful or salty, call upon the waters of the great flood.

SAUSAGE GRAVY

This gravy summoning takes some preparation. You either need to have seitan made, or have some vegan sausage patty crumbles (or other vegan meat) from the portal you know as the grocery store.

1. Begin as all of the gravy incantations begin, but with one slight change. Melt some vegan butter in a pan and first sauté small chunks of seitan (or vegan sausage or TVP).

2. After it is browned, cast a small handful of flour into the pot. Upon the browning of the flour, bring forth some high-fat coconut milk into the cauldron. This will be incredibly thick. Thin it out with vegetable broth to the desired consistency. Season with salt and pepper. Boil like a bubbling muck for several minutes.

ROASTED GARLIC GRAVY

This gravy summoning also takes significant preparation. Whenever you roast anything in life, make some fucking roasted garlic (see page 144). You are going to use it anyway. If you do not, you are a fool.

1. Begin this ritual like all other gravy rituals. Heat up a heart-attack amount of vegan butter in a pot. In the summoning crucible should be a small amount of flour along with the roasted garlic. Sauté for a minute until the flour has browned to the dark side.

2. A quick pour of soy sauce, a dash of pepper and Italian seasoning, along with vegetable broth shall you boil in this cauldron of might. Simmer until thick.

If the flavors intensify beyond your ability to enjoy the dark presence, douse this beast with water.

THREE BEAN CHILI

SPELL REAGENTS (INGREDIENTS)

- Can of chickpeas
- Can of kidney beans
- Can of black beans
- Can of corn *(optional)*
- Chili powder
- Cayenne pepper
- Salt
- Pepper
- Several cloves of fresh garlic *(and/or garlic powder)*
- Whatever herbs you want or a premade Italian seasoning
- Vegan red wine *(optional)*
- Bell peppers
- Onion
- Tomato
- A small amount of tomato sauce
- Cilantro
- Canned chipotle peppers or chipotle powder *(optional, but fucking do it)*
- Olive oil
- Vegetable broth *(optional)*

Chili of Northern Darkness

The fall of mankind will have one savior. In the desolation of the end, a burning phoenix will rise. This phoenix will smell of a spicy mixture of chipotle, chili, and cayenne pepper…

Religions and cults around the world have held the number three in sacred adoration for ages. In the depths of your infernal soul, you feel the power of this number. Yet few know that the burning desire is really for three bean chili!

Anything involving three to four cans will be a fuckton of food in general. What do you do with all of this food? Try all the alternative ways of eating chili at the end of this spell, lest you get bored of eating chili.

1. This starts by drowning some onions in a good bit of olive oil. Go heavy on the oil; you will be making a shitload of chili. Sauté the onions for just a few minutes. They should be shiny and fresh like a virgin sacrifice, not like a shriveled ancient corpse.

2. Add your chopped bell peppers and your optional can of drained corn (no corn in the picture) and proceed to cook these implements of sacrifice for another minute or so. Again, the goal is not to cook the soul out of them. They have already sold their soul anyways.

3. Before this next step, make sure you have drained and rinsed your beans. The easiest way to do this is to empty the can into a spiked colander and run them under the waters of eternal life.

   Though I do not object to "bean can water" in some things, it has no place in the sacred circle of this pot. So pour forth your drained and rinsed beans into your onion and bell pepper mixture. Summon the chopped tomatoes into this cauldron. It is not so obvious from the picture how many tomatoes were added, so put in three or four small/medium ones or however many you have. It is a great way to use up all of your ripe tomatoes which are about to go bad. Stir the mixture with perfect spirals of the gods. CONTINUED

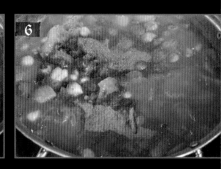

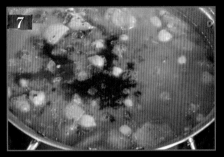

4. Now we must get the juices flowing on everything. Add in a small amount of pasta sauce to bring the "water" element into this concoction. Any very basic pasta sauce will do. Stir this in! It is almost time to spice it!

5. At this stage, we add the flavor of existence that will flow throughout and make the whole ritual worthy of the dark gods. In the picture you see salt and pepper, garlic powder (or grate several cloves of fresh garlic), dried herbs of your choice (or pre-made Italian seasoning blend), and chipotle peppers (optional). You do know that you can add whatever the hell you want, right? These are just the concepts. Get creative, make this shit your own. Get an inspiration from the beyond.

6. Why the fuck do we call this chili? Because there is chili powder in it. Get that shit in there. I also like to invoke cayenne pepper to add an additional kind of heat. You can call upon fresh chilies, jalapeños, habaneros, or fucking whatever.

7. I like to add a bloodstain of vegan red wine. This goes well with almost any tomato saucy spell.

8. Cover, reduce heat and simmer for about 20-30 minutes. If it sits around on no heat or very low heat after this it will only get better. Like an ancient undead Lich, it gets better with time.

9. Upon five minutes before the consumption, stir in a large handful of cilantro.

Your final creation arises from the beyond!

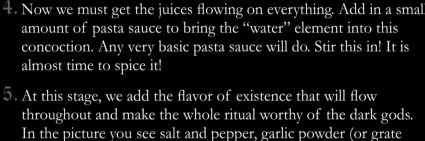

NOW THAT YOU HAVE MORE CHILI THAN YOU CAN STAND...
TRY THESE VARIATIONS:

Chili Cheese Dogs

Chili Cheese Fries

Chili Cheese Burrito

Chili Cheese Pasta

Chili Cheese Burger

You get the idea. Succumb to the obsession.

GET STARTED

What are you putting off in life? Waiting until everything is perfect? Waiting until things are just a little better? Stop waiting and do at least one thing towards your goals.

It will never all be perfect. You do not wait until everything is perfect to drive a long distance. Even in the dark, all you need to know is the destination, possible routes, and that your headlights will let you know what is immediately in front of you. With just this information, you can drive all the way across your country. All you need to know about your goals are possible routes, the next action to take on those routes, and the gas (motivation) to take the next step.

What is the one thing you can do to get started on your goals? Even if roads are blocked and you are forced to take different routes than you first intended...know that as long as there is a way, the next action is all that is needed and all that you can do.

ANY BEAN BURGERS

SPELL REAGENTS (INGREDIENTS)

- **Any beans** *(canned or softened from dry beans)*
- **Panko** *(Japanese bread crumbs)*
- **Cornstarch**
- **Spices** *(anything you think would be good in a burger)*
- **Cooking oil**
- **Water**

This is so goddamn fucking easy. You can go from the unholy depths of a can of beans to the divine heights of burgers in 10-15 minutes.

Forces of Bean Burger Storms

Do you have what it takes to make this happen? You do not need to be one of the chosen; however, you do need some panko and cornstarch. If you are not buying panko already, seriously, what the fuck are you doing? This shit is so versatile and amazing that you will be regretting the wasted years of your life.

Buy panko at the Asian store; it's way fucking cheaper than in the regular grocery store. Sometimes the panko in non-Asian stores is not vegan! Fuck that shit. Go to the Asian store, buy a big-ass bag of panko and prepare for victory.

1. Begin this spell with a can of drained and rinsed beans in your summoning bowl. It does not matter what beans have been chosen. Just get some fucking beans and make it happen. Mash the beans with your mace, or potato masher, or whatever the hell will get the mashing job done. Call forth your panko breadcrumbs. Add a fistful of panko. It should be about 1/5 or so the amount of beans. The exact quantity is not important…just do it!

2. Prepare some cornstarch in a bowl. Not too much, just a bit. Add a small amount of water to it so that it is very thick. Add just a bit more water to the point where it becomes thin and easy to stir. The whole concept is to add just enough water to dampen the panko.

CONTINUED

3. Pour like a trickle of blood off a minor wound upon the panko. Mix everything together into a semi-thick paste. Now you must spice this paste! Beans are fucking bland on their own. Add whatever the hell you think would be good in a burger. Salt, pepper, onion powder, chili powder, various spice mixes, soup broth, Creole seasoning, dried herbs, etc. Pick a few and spice it until it looks spiced. Start with tried and true shit so you realize how good this is, then you can fuck it up in whatever horrid way you like. Remember the original rule of cooking…it does not need everything in the fucking world.

4. The dark gods command that you form the beans into a shape. Choose the form of the beans and be destroyed! Burgers, dog, pentagrams, whatever. Form them, and heat some oil in a pan on a medium high heat. Sauté on both sides until browned. If the whim takes you, toss some spices on the outside to encrust with blackened spice char.

That is it! Put on an epic bun with vegan mayonnaise, sriracha, mustard and whatever the hell else. Your final torment awaits.

WHAT EXCITES YOU IN LIFE?

A great author named Tim Ferris said in his book *The Four Hour Work Week*: don't ask, "What do you want?" Ask, "What excites you?" If you ask, "What do you want," many people don't really know. They spout off wishes and hopes about health, wealth, and love, but nothing that would have them take action. A far better question to stimulate action is, "What excites us in life?"

So what excites you? What gets you out of bed in the morning? The answer to this question is at least a concrete one. It gets the emotions stirring. The only way to accomplish anything extraordinary in life is to get emotionally excited about it. There will be serious hurdles to overcome in anything that you do. The only thing that will keep you going after the first or second hurdle will be your level of excitement.

MASHED POTATOES

Curse You All Potatoes

SPELL REAGENTS
(INGREDIENTS)

- Brown potatoes
- Red potatoes
- Vegan butter
- Coconut, almond, or your favorite nut milk
- Salt
- Pepper
- Green onion
- Garlic powder

You have to be some kind of asshole not to like mashed potatoes. I mean, fucking really. Partake with a summoning of gravy, toasted atop a pile of spiced vegan meats in a shepherd's pie, or simply alone, barren, and perfect. CONTINUED

21

1. An ancient secret to the mashed potato ritual is the invoking of a mixture of potatoes. Here, in this spell, I am using both baking potatoes and red potatoes.

Rend their skin from their bodies. Or don't, I don't give a shit. You will just have plenty of potato skin in the mashed potatoes. Choose your fate wisely and according to your temperament.

2. Draw and quarter the potato pieces. Drop their remains in lightly salted boiling waters of this earth. They are fully tortured and ready for confession when easily pierced with the mystical knife.

3. Drain the waters of life, and mix with nut milk and a large amount of vegan butter. Mash together with the fury of your soul.

Spice with salt, a bit of pepper, even less garlic powder, and thin slices of green onion. Mix like the alchemists of old.

BONUS: FRIED MASHED POTATO BALLS

4. Gather a handful of mashed potatoes into a ball. Compress it with the weight of giants to make sure it is dense. This is not that big of a fucking deal, just compact it a bit. Roll them around in the cornstarch of the ages. Deep fry until awesome.

RICE PILAF

Ricebound, by the Devil

SPELL REAGENTS (INGREDIENTS)

- **Rice** *(either long grain or parboiled rice)*
- **Vegetable broth**
- **Spices** *(salt, pepper, any spice blend or selection of spices – optional)*
- **Olive oil, vegan butter, or canola oil**

There is so much suffering and torment when it comes to making basic rice. Follow this method precisely and you shall be victorious without fail.

This will make a flavorful pile of rice corpses to be used in many rituals. If the dish itself is tremendous in salt and spices…use temperance when preparing the rice.

1. Bring two parts vegetable broth and a quick pour of olive oil for every part of rice to a bubbling boil. If the portents augur it, add some spices.

2. The rice shall be cast in now and not before! Cover, reduce heat to low, and simmer as if the end times have come. In about 15-20 minutes or when all water is absorbed…remove from the heat and let sit.

Its glory shall reign for ever and ever.

BISCUITS

SPELL REAGENTS (INGREDIENTS)

- Self-rising flour
- High-fat coconut milk *(can)*
- Vinegar
- Sugar
- Vegan butter

What is more tempting in this world than flaky, divinely perfect biscuits? Though it seems strange, we shall invoke our own buttermilk substitute with vinegar and coconut milk. Fear not the vinegar. Your biscuits will not taste like vinegar. These biscuits come out amazing.

You will fucking shit yourself.

A Biscuit Forlorn

1. Invoke a quick pour of vinegar to some coconut milk. Don't freak out over exactly how much, just get some vinegar in there. Let it fester for about ten minutes while you scour for your other ingredients. Pour melted vegan butter into the vinegar milk as if you were scalding the hordes attacking your castle. Use about a quarter as much melted vegan butter than the amount of coconut milk.

2. Mix in self-rising flour to make a dough. A bit of sugar tempts the daemons of taste. Keep adding self-rising flour until it is not sticky like a quagmire of life. Knead the dough well. Don't freak out about how much. It will work.

3. Form the dough into large biscuits. This shit rises a bit, but don't expect it to grow to unearthly sizes.

   Pour a mixture of coconut milk and melted vegan butter upon them. Do not skip this step. It gives the outside a perfect texture as well as a diabolically beaconing color.

Bake at 450° F (230° C) for about 15 minutes or until done.

BUFFALO SEITAN BITES

SPELL REAGENTS (INGREDIENTS)

- **Cooking oil**
- **Seitan**
- **Buffalo sauce**
- **Cayenne pepper** *(optional)*
- **Vegan butter**

Buffalo sauce (which does not come from buffaloes) is a cayenne pepper-based hot sauce. While not as burning hot as the flames of the sun, its fire burns brighter with additional cayenne pepper. In this world, not all Buffalo sauces are created equal.

If you live in the U.S., I highly recommend Frank's Wing Sauce™ as the solid go-to Buffalo sauce. The "natural butter-type flavor" in the ingredients is vegan (at the time of this writing). If this no longer exists in the future, we live in a desolate world in which it is probably not worth living. It would be best to go into a state of mourning. As a partial alternative, you can try all of the Buffalo sauces in your sad excuse of an existence and rejoice in the best one. There really is no other way.

*The company mentioned does not endorse this book or the Vegan Black Metal Chef project.

The Seitan Bites Offering

The conjuring of the Buffalo seitan bites is simplicity itself; however, there is one dark, perilous trap. You must sauté the seitan sufficiently or else the whole thing goes to crap.

1. The first step is to heat up the cooking oil upon your pan. The oil should reflect in it the grim darkness of your dungeon.

2. Place the chopped up seitan in the heated oil. Seriously, take some time to brown this. When it is starting to look a little brown, keep going. It should not be burnt or blackened, for this is an abomination. But it should be browned well in parts. Let the heat of chaos transform this pile of spongy brains into crispy-on-the-outside deliciousness.

◄ The transformation takes place as shown. Those who have eyes feast upon its glory.

3. When fully browned, add the Buffalo sauce, vegan butter, and additional cayenne pepper. You know how freakishly hot you want it. Dash on the cayenne pepper with reckless abandon!

4. Stir this around, and cook for another minute or two. Serve with blasphemous vegan ranch dressing.

MAKE YOUR OWN SEITAN

Look, I am not a purist when it comes to food. Don't reinvent the wheel if the wheel is already good and cheap. Except for specialty seitan that might be a pain, make that shit yourself. A lot of the store-bought seitan just does not cook the same as self-made. I have no idea why. They are just different. Seitan is also ridiculously cheap and easy to make, yet somewhat expensive to buy. So make that shit when you are not hungry and are going to be home doing something else for an hour. This will make a week's worth of seitan for pennies. See the Vegan Meats section on page 202.

JAMBALAYA

SPELL REAGENTS (INGREDIENTS)

- **Rice** *(use parboiled long grain rice for perfect look and texture)*
- **Creole or Cajun seasoning**
- **Onion powder**
- **Garlic powder**
- **Black pepper**
- **Paprika**
- **Habanero pepper**

- **Vegetable broth**
- **Olive oil**
- **Bell pepper**
- **Tomato**
- **Tomato paste** *(optional)*
- **Onion**
- **Some kind of vegan meat like seitan and/or vegan shrimp**

Where Jambalaya Angels Lie

From the hells of the Cajun world comes a dish that is both tasty, easy and fearsome. The habanero pepper will give you a kick in the ass if the gods have imbued it with extra fire. Prepare a pot and a pan for this rite. The rice and meats will be called into this realm separately, and then combined in the end.

Prepare for this by cutting up the onions, bell pepper, tomato, and habanero pepper into squares. Don't use the seeds of the habanero unless you are ready for hellfire.

1. Sauté the onions in olive oil over a medium heat until slightly brown. Fucking easy!

2. Throw the bell peppers and tomato into the cauldron. The bell peppers should become slightly crisp with a possible blackened spot upon them. The tomatoes should weep down like a tortured soul.

3. Now to add the fire and spice. I like an entire habanero pepper for one cup of rice. It will come out fairly spicy, but not deathly hot. Time to enchant this pot with the Creole seasoning, onion powder, garlic powder, paprika, black pepper and tomato paste. The highest proportion by far should be the Creole seasoning. Everything else can be sprinkled in like fairy mist. CONTINUED

4. Now call upon the vegetable broth and rice. I use twice as much vegetable broth as rice. You can add a scorpion pinch more water to make the rice softer. Less will make it firmer. Bring this to a boil, cover, reduce heat to low and simmer like the cycles of life and death have no meaning.

5. Sauté some vegan meat, seitan, or whatever the hell in your other pot. I also use olive oil for this so it does not taste fucked up when mixed into the rice. If sautéing seitan, make sure it is well browned on all sides. Curse your creation with a spatter of Creole seasoning. Not too much! It will become too salty.

6. Lo! The rice is done! Combine your two blasphemous concoctions and serve with a side of misanthropy.

THE RELATIVE AND THE ULTIMATE

There are two ways to see everything in the world. The relative, temporary, "everyday" standpoint and the ultimate, "eternal" standpoint. Reality is the seemingly paradoxical merger of the two. In the context of veganism, the relative truth is that most animals raised for food live in complete hell their entire lives. The best part of their lives is when they are put to death. In the ultimate sense, there are no such things as morals. All actions just are. The Relative reality reminds us to try our hardest to help those animals and humans whose lives are in constant hell. It helps us cultivate compassion and action. The Ultimate reality gives us a broad philosophical perspective to remain stable in our work and life. Living too much in the Relative reality breeds anger and depression. Living too much in the Ultimate reality makes us aloof, lethargic, and cold. Remember to think about both halves of the truth when considering something. Both halves of the truth are equally as true. Balance must be found between the two for your life.

BRUSSELS SPROUTS SAUTÉED IN TRUFFLE OIL

EURO-AMERICAN ✕

Obscure Brussels Sprouts For the Multiverse

SPELL REAGENTS (INGREDIENTS)

- **Canola** *(or other neutral cooking oil)*
- **Brussels sprouts**
- **Salt**
- **Pepper**
- **Black truffle oil**
- **Mushrooms** *(optional)*
- **Bell pepper** *(optional)*

Most of the time, addictions ruin lives. They break apart families, lead to suicide, or in the case of religion…the slaughter of multitudes.

Sometimes addiction is eternally blissful. Such is the case with Brussels sprouts sautéed in truffle oil with salt and pepper.

CONTINUED

31

You may think, "Fuck, I fucking hate those fucking bitter-ass mini cabbages." I would agree with this statement in most cases. Preparing them in this sacred way shall reverse this thought in your mind.

Everyone says their way of making Brussels sprouts is the best. But seriously, this is fucking amazing. If it sucks, you can throw this book away, burn it, and talk shit about me all over the internet and I will agree on every post saying I knowingly lied to you.

Simplicity is best. The flavor of the truffle oil along with the individual ingredients is very strong. The only spices this needs are salt and pepper. It does need plenty of salt and pepper. So don't skimp on that shit.

In preparation of this dish, cut the bottoms off all your Brussels sprouts, remove the top two leaves or so, and cut the remainder in half or in quarters if very large.

1. Heat some neutral cooking oil in a pan on medium heat. Too hot and they will burn too fast before they cook all the way through.

2. Add your Brussels sprouts, sauté them for a decent little while. They begin to brown like the ass of Satan.

3. At this point, begin to add copious amounts of pepper and a good bit of salt. A decent bit of both; however, absolutely more pepper than salt. You can always add more salt in the end. The pepper will begin to blacken on the sprouts. You should start singing the song "Blackened" by Metallica as you sauté them further.

4. Add your mushrooms and bell peppers, and more salt and pepper. The combined tastes of all will be phenomenal.

5. Here is the most critical step. It may take a time of practice to get it exactly to your taste. It is time to add the truffle oil. How much depends on many factors. Some truffle oil is much stronger than others. If it is very potent, open the bottle and pour a quick line across the sautéing food, then another line like an X.

   Truffle oil can be very powerful and tasty, but can be easily overdone. If the truffle oil does not kick you in the face with flavor, then it may need more.

Sauté till the Brussels sprouts are fairly blackened in parts, and taste them to make sure they are done. Sometimes they are not cooked all the way through. Reduce the heat if burning and cook for longer. Add additional salt, pepper or truffle oil as needed.

6

◀ It should look like this when near done.

Serve upon a rice pilaf (see page 23) as a meal in itself or as a side dish. It is glorious and addictive.

SUCCESS IS NOT ABSOLUTE, FAILURE IS NOT FATAL

Learn to humbly enjoy success and recover from failure. Oftentimes a single success is not ever-sustaining, just as a failure is not an absolute end. It is what one does daily or weekly, on a consistent basis, that really matters in life. It is this consistent compounding increase that really begins to change your life dramatically over time.

What does this mean? If you get 0.5% better at something daily, the same little bit of increase three years from now will yield much more results than the 0.5% at the beginning. The effects start off slow, then increase exponentially over time. If you get better at your chosen skills in life, or if you accomplish more of your goals in life, the gains made from these grow upon themselves day after day. This works in both directions. If your life goes a small amount in a direction you do not wish to go, this will compound over time just as going in the direction you want to go. Consciously pick a direction in life. If you go a little this way, then a little that way, then back again, the effects of your actions can not accumulate. You are choosing a direction whether or not you choose it consciously. This same power can help you take flight in life, or become a crushing weight. It is up to you and it is never too late.

SIMPLE ROASTED VEGETABLES

SPELL REAGENTS (INGREDIENTS)

- **Many types of vegetables will do** *(I am using potato, carrot, & onion)*
- **Spices** *(dried herbs and other spices)*
- **Olive oil**
- **Salt and pepper** *(if not included above)*

Roasting in the fires of hell, slowly in a pool of fat. Who would have thought this death would be so glorious for almost all vegetables involved? Potatoes with a just slightly crisp outer layer, yet moist, tender innards. Robust carrots teeming with flavor. Onions that cause the tears of a thousand villages. Tears of fear and wonder.

Roasted Roots, Bloody Roots

Roasted vegetables will be served during the end times. That is how damn good they are.

Though it is tempting to add every vegetable ever to this hell roast, heed the original warning of the elder gods: "More will fuck things up fast." Some vegetables will add too much water content to this dish and make your life a soggy flood of misery.

1. Cut some potatoes and carrots into a pan. Spice the fuck out of them. There are two things to remember with these roasted vegetables. First, do not be afraid of oil. Second, fear many things, but do not fear spices. It should bathe in a pool of fat and spice. I used salt, pepper, Italian seasoning (dried herb blend), additional rosemary, Cajun seasoning, a "hamburger" spice blend, and a touch of chili powder. Use whatever the hell you want, just use plenty of it. Mix together to distribute the spices over all, like a communist spice intervention.

2. Place this pan in your oven at between 350-400° Fahrenheit (180-205° C). Scorch them for about 40-50 minutes, stirring once or twice. Take your sacrificial pan out and add the onion and additional spices.

3. Continue the oven torture for another 20 minutes. In the last 5-7 minutes press the broil button and broil on high. Here is where you must be as watchful as the evil eye. Invoking the broiler causes everything to have a diabolically crisp surface, yet can quickly turn your entire dish to char. Watch carefully but let the fire daemons work their magic.

The simplicity is unbelievable.

GERMAN POTATO SALAD

SPELL REAGENTS (INGREDIENTS)

- **Red potatoes**
- **Olive oil**
- **Red wine vinegar**
- **Red onion**
- **Italian seasoning**
- **Mustard**
- **Salt**

One must search the icy peaks of the North for the finest party dishes in the world. The attributes of such a noble dish are thus: inexpensive, makes a lot of food, does not take much work, and tastes fucking amazing. When you bring this feast, the commoners at such a gathering will have no choice but to bow down in your divine presence.

1. Start by scalding your potatoes in a vat of salted boiling liquid, preferably water.

The Fall of German Potato Salad Dominion

2. Whilst the potatoes endure their hot bath, prepare the foundation of your sauce. It begins by pouring a skull's worth of olive oil into a bowl.

3. Proceed with the addition of approximately one quarter or a bit more of red wine vinegar as you used oil. There is leeway in this amount. Just approximate it and learn the truths of your own taste.

4. Squirt two slit-wrists worth of mustard into this mixture.

5. Finish by adding some Italian seasoning, red onion, and a bit of salt. Use temperance when adding the Italian seasoning.

6. Add many thin crescents of sliced red onion. Do not be shy at this stage, you should cry with the tears of a universe torn apart.

7. Stir this up into a whirring oblivion.

8. When the potato innards are soft, pour this concoction of tortured souls upon them. Salt their wounds thoroughly.

Serve almost as cold as the unfrozen depths of hell, yet do not freeze it! Do not neglect this step lest all be lost.

Remember this: if potatoes are ever summoned, they call for some salt. Coat thoroughly and place in a storage sarcophagus. Place this in the freezer for 30 minutes or until chilled (but not frozen).

VEGAN RANCH DRESSING

SPELL REAGENTS (INGREDIENTS)

- **Vegan mayonnaise**
- **Salt**
- **Pepper**
- **White vinegar**
- **Onion powder**
- **Onion flakes**

- **Dill** *(I usually use dry but you can also use fresh)*
- **Fakon bits** *(any brand, optional)*
- **Parsley flakes** *(I usually use dry but you can use fresh)*

The entire cost of this cookbook or ebook is covered in this way of making vegan ranch dressing. This shit is amazing, and is amazing on everything. A deal has been made with the devil itself to bring you this blasphemy. So value your soul since I sold mine.

Nebular Ranch Dressing Winter

As awesome as this tastes, it is simple as fuck to make. Do not worry about exact amounts of each ingredient. Just put a bit of each thing in, use the photos, and your common sense. There is a huge range of "right," so just do it and don't freak out about it. Take this shit to the next level by adding your favorite brand of Fakon Bits. There are several brands of "bacon flavored chips" made out of soy and totally vegan in most grocery store salad dressing aisles.

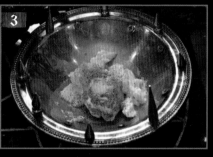

What the hell are you still looking at this for? Begin to combine the ingredients!

1. This ritual starts with a few scoops of vegan mayonnaise. Even vegans can enjoy the decadent pleasures of whipped fat.

2. Add copious amounts of blacker than black pepper.

3. Sprinkle the salt of the earth into the spawning bowl.

4. Pour forth the garlic powder upon your summoning.

5. The onion flakes and onion powder are welcomed into your dish.

6. The dill beckons with its fragrance from the beyond.

7. The green bits are parsley, add some for more green specks.

Finalize this spell by adding just enough vinegar to make it a bit liquidy. Go easy here; too little is better than too much.

PROCESSED COMMERCIAL VEGAN CHEESE SAUCE

SPELL REAGENTS (INGREDIENTS)

- **Some type of vegan cheese** *(think cheddar, American, or mozzarella etc... just not "fancy cheese")*
- **Coconuts, almond, rice, cashew or soy milk** *(or whatever vegan milk)*
- **Vegan butter**
- **Sriracha** *(for nacho style sauce)*

Commercial Cheese Sauce Torn Asunder

This simple incantation opens the doors to endless alchemy. This works in cohort with countless other rituals. The summoning of nachos, chili cheese dogs, mac and cheese, and more require the quintessence of this base summoning.

1. Begin by spilling the blood of your favorite vegan milk. I am partial to coconut milk for this, but any will do. All will taste slightly different, so see which ones call to your being. Place a decent amount of your vegan cheddar or other cheese (shreds, slices or blocks) within the blood of the fallen vegan milk.

   Do not forsake the vegan butter. The final outcome shall look fatally similar with or without adding this, yet will taste drastically and dreadfully different. Add a blasphemously sized chunk of the semi-solid vegan butter gold. Squirt in a stream of sriracha as if it were pulsating out of a punctured aorta (if making a spicy nacho sauce).

2. Bring this sacred liquid to a boil, reduce heat to low and simmer for a few minutes until it is one like demonic souls twisting in the abyss.

3. Your final product should taste as sinfully decadent as it appears!

RICE OF THE REALM (EURO-AMERICAN)

Parboiled long grain rice or long grain rice. To get that perfect texture in many things, the parboiled long grain rice will be your lord and savior. It has a unique taste and texture. Regular long grain rice will also work its magic in the dishes of this section.

*The company in this picture does not endorse this book or the Vegan Black Metal Chef project.

NACHO PEANUT QUESO SAUCE

SPELL REAGENTS (INGREDIENTS)

- **Peanuts or cashews** *(salted or unsalted – any store-bought variety that is vegan)*
- **Vegetable broth**
- **Nutritional yeast**
- **Tomato paste**
- **Sriracha**
- **Garlic powder**
- **Chili powder** *(optional)*
- **Neutral oil like canola oil**
- **Any red-colored spices like smoked or regular paprika** *(optional)*
- **Salt**

Calling this "cheese" is not exactly accurate. It does not taste like an American-style cheese. It tastes like awesome sorta queso dip, yet versatile enough to be used in many things. This arcane magic makes a diabolical mac 'n' cheese, nachos, sandwich or potato topping. Whatever blasphemous name it is given, it is amazing and addictive.

The hardest fucking part about this dish is just deciding to soak some peanuts overnight. It does not matter how many peanuts. Even but a handful of nuts makes a good amount. Just fucking do it. Get off your ass and soak some peanuts now.

Quesophetamine

1. Summon your soaked peanuts into your blender of oblivion.

2. If the fates have decided you to use powdered vegetable broth, it will look like Picture 2. If not, skip this step. The liquid vegetable broth will be the water added at the end.

3. Call upon a bit of nutritional yeast, whispered in legend and held sacred amongst the vegan community.

4. The tomato paste is symbolic of the bloodstain that is society.

5. Add garlic powder, sriracha, chili powder and anything else red. Paprika, smoked paprika, roasted red peppers…all or none of it. This will aid in its glorious appearance.

6. Do not neglect this step…fear not the oil. Summon a good bit of oil into the blender, and pour forth water enough to blend.

7. Blend like the swirling of a thousand winds.

8. Pour this putrid liquid in a pot, bring to a boil, cover, reduce heat and simmer in the darkness of space for ten minutes. The final moments may need salt. Use the detectors on your tongue to divine the truth.

Alas, the simmering forges an unholy alliance of flavor. It is ready to do your bidding.

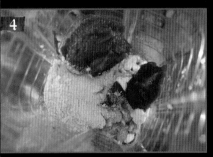

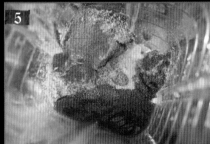

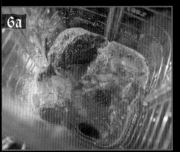

Oracle of Inspiration

Roasted Potatoes

SPELL REAGENTS (INGREDIENTS)

- Potatoes
- Olive oil
- Spices

The more vegetables you roast, the more shit changes. There is something special in the purity of roasting just potatoes.

The roasted potatoes themselves can be used as ingredients in other dishes.

Follow the same concepts as the roasted root vegetables (page 34), but just use potatoes.

Do not be afraid of spices. Spice the fuck out of them. This is where most people fail.

Americana Mac and Cheese

SPELL REAGENTS (INGREDIENTS)

- Pasta
- Commercial vegan cheese
- Vegan butter
- Nut milk
- Salt

Boil the pasta in lightly salted water until done. Strain the pasta and discard the water. Put the pasta in the same pot back on the stove over medium heat.

Add the commercial vegan cheese (page 40), a bit of nut milk, and a good bit of vegan butter.

Melt everything together and stir for mac and cheese unholy glory.

Scan for updates.

Oracle of Inspiration

Cole Slaw

SPELL REAGENTS (INGREDIENTS)

- Red cabbage
- Green cabbage
- Carrots
- Vegan mayonnaise
- White vinegar
- Salt
- Pepper
- Dill
- Onion powder

Slice up some of each cabbage into thin strips. Chop a carrot into thin sticks or use a potato peeler to peel off thin strips of carrot. Mix together the other ingredients like in the vegan ranch dressing in a separate bowl. Combine and chill for the ultimate slaw.

Eat a Goddamn Salad

SPELL REAGENTS (INGREDIENTS)

- Things you would put in a salad
- Vegan meat (optional)
- Salt
- Fat

You know what makes a salad great? Salt and fat. For the salt, add some chips, potato sticks, or other salty snack. For the fat, toss in a rich dressing. The ranch in this chapter (page 38) is utterly phenomenal. I like salads, but I do not need to teach you eight million ways to make a salad.

Eat Some Fucking Fruit

SPELL REAGENTS (INGREDIENTS)

- Fruit

Eat some fucking fruit as a meal. It should go without saying that every meal does not have to be vegan grilled cheese yuba bacon cheeseburgers. Yes, for an entire meal, eat some fucking fruit. This concludes the fully raw section of the book.

Oracle of Inspiration

Shepherd's Pie

SPELL REAGENTS (INGREDIENTS)

- Potatoes
- Vegan butter
- Vegan milk *(any nut milk that you like)*
- Salt
- Pepper
- Garlic powder
- Green onion *(optional)*
- Vegan meat
- Mushrooms
- Onions
- Chilies *(optional)*
- Spices *(those above, any spice blends that seem right for Euro-American spiced meats)*

This combines the concepts of mashed potatoes (page 21) and sautéing vegan meats such as in the nachos and tacos of the Hispanic & Latino section (page 88). Instead of using taco/Hispanic seasonings use more Euro-American seasonings…or do whatever the hell you want. Otherwise it is the same concept. Spread the sautéed vegan meat on a baking pan. Smear a lot of mashed potatoes on top. The mashed potatoes need to lessen the flavor impact of the spiced meats, mushrooms, and onions. Use plenty of potatoes. Put in the oven and set it to broil on high. Toast the top of the mashed potatoes. Do not leave this unwatched for long. When it looks perfect, it is done.

Potato Salad

SPELL REAGENTS (INGREDIENTS)

- Potatoes
- Vegan mayonnaise
- White vinegar
- Mustard
- Dill
- Garlic powder
- Salt
- Pepper
- Sliced green onion and/or celery

Use the same concept as the vegan ranch dressing (page 38) but with the ingredients above. Skin (or don't) some potatoes, boil them until done. Set aside and let cool for a minute.

Mix the above ingredients in a spiked bowl. Use only a squirt of mustard. Do not go crazy with it. Add the potatoes and cool in your refrigerator.

This is potato salad perfection.

Oracle of Inspiration

Philly Cheese Steak

SPELL REAGENTS (INGREDIENTS)

- Seitan or chickun-style seitan *(or another appropriate vegan meat)*
- Vegan cheese *(either commercial vegan cheese or the nut cheese from this book)*
- Onions
- Peppers
- Mushrooms *(optional)*
- Spices *(salt, pepper, chili powder, Italian seasoning, or any appropriate spice blend)*
- French bread *(or other good bread)*

A vegan Philly will always make everyone jealous as fuck. Vegan meat, sautéed onions and peppers, and vegan cheese sauce makes this shit happen like nothing else. Cut the seitan into strips and follow the concepts of sautéing the seitan well such as in the fajitas recipe (page 106). After the seitan is well browned, add the onions and peppers. Spice the fuck out of them. Process the commercial vegan cheese as called forth on page 40. You can make the nut cheese instead (page 42) if you wish. Toast some French bread, put on your vegan meats, vegetables, and cheese.

Ingest the ultimate sandwich.

Yuba Bacon Seitan Cheeseburgers

SPELL REAGENTS (INGREDIENTS)

- Yuba
- Everything you need for bacon sauce
- Maple syrup
- Soy sauce
- Liquid smoke
- Onion powder
- Salt
- Pepper
- Garlic powder
- Canola oil *(or any other oil)*
- Vegan butter
- Everything you need for Processed Vegan Cheese Sauce
- Either commercial vegan cheese or Peanut Queso Cheese Sauce
- Seitan or chickun-style seitan
- Bread
- Anything you would put on a sandwich

Make the yuba bacon with the yuba bacon methods (page 210). Slice the seitan thin and sauté a few slices of your dark lord and master. Make the grilled cheese sandwiches using the quesadilla methods (page 113). Make the processed cheese sauce using the vegan cheese sauce method (page 40). Pile everything into an epic burger.

Introduction – Asian

Ahhhhhh. The taste of American-bastardized Asian cooking. From the land of mystic dragons, the fine inventors of tofu and seitan have taught us many mysteries from the beyond.

This refers to East Asian cooking, you fool…not Indian Asian or Russian Asian cooking.

Of course this will not be traditional. Tradition is for the mindless sway of the zombified masses. Your hell-forged mind already knows this.

The first and main concept you will be using in most, if not all, of these dishes is the "three pot method." This means that you will have three pots before you as you do most of these summoning rites: a pot for the vegetables and vegan meats, a pot for the noodles or rice, and a pot for the sauce to be made. These all come together at the end to keep the vegetables diabolically crisp and give you maniacal control over the sauce.

This seems trivial, yet will make more difference than anything else you do in this section.

Heed its words, mortal.

PREMADE ASIAN SAUCES

In this chapter, you will learn the secrets of making many Asian sauces from "scratch." However, as you wander the aisles of Asian stores, you will see torrents of premade sauce bottles, several of which are vegan!

As you may have learned by buying a bottle of teriyaki or other "stir fry" sauce from a store, oftentimes these sauces are decent, but do not really get you to restaurant quality.

You will learn in this chapter how to make many Asian meals with a vegetable broth base (see page 61). You will still use that vegetable broth along with these sauces. However, the sauces will act as a substitute for adding the soy sauce and some other spices.

You cannot completely know what these will taste like before you try them. Some you will like, some you will not. After you find the ones you like, you can adjust the methods to maximize your deliciousness.

*The companies in this picture do not endorse this book or the Vegan Black Metal Chef project.

PAD THAI

Thus Spake the Pad Thai Spirit

SPELL REAGENTS (INGREDIENTS)

- **Tofu** *(extra firm or firm)*
- **Bean sprouts**
- **A tomato**
- **Peanuts** *(salted or unsalted)*
- **Sriracha and chili powder**
- **Garlic and garlic powder**
- **Green onions**
- **Sugar** *(turbinado sugar - "sugar in the raw" or a vegan white sugar)*

- **Tamarind paste**
- **Salt**
- **Rice noodles**
- **Cilantro**
- **A lime**
- **Vinegar**
- **Peanut butter**

Behold the Glorious Pad Thai! For those who have followed me from the beginning, this is the dark ritual heard 'round the world. What arcane mysteries does this dish hold for those who dare to partake of its essence? Why have so many attempted this in the ancient past and met with naught but failure? What devil beguiles the actions of mortals who venture into this realm?

The keys are in the methodology, for there are very few actual cooking steps.

  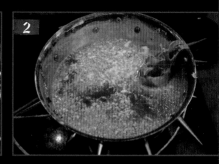

PRE-PREPARATION:

Start your tofu pressing by following the steps in the pressing tofu section (Vegan Meats, page 194). You will want to crush your peanuts in advance with the fury of the ancients. I accomplish this by taking two plastic bags (using only one will rip), pouring a fiendish amount of peanuts in the first bag, encapsulating that bag within the space dimension of another bag, then with the soul of a barbarian, begin to crush those peanuts with any massive object in your reach. A pot, a mace, a rolling pin, a hammer, anything you can brutally kill someone with that has no sharp edges will do. Crush the peanuts into a fine powder. Settle not for half crushed peanuts, they will thwart your attempts.

Submerge your rice noodles in a bowl or pan of room-temperature water. Take pleasure out of pretending to drown your enemies in this step. They will get a little soft while you make the sauce, but the centers will stay firm and turgid. You will be basing the amount of ingredients in the sauce around the amount of rice noodles you will be using. The concept here is that the rice noodles are as bland as tasting the unmanifest and need to be heavily spiced. The pictures show an approximate amount for about 1/2 lb of rice noodles (1/2 of a package sold here).

Cut up a medium-size tomato into medium-sized chunks. Do not lend your obsessive compulsive mind to the size; it matters not. Decapitate a few green onions and cut them into little stalks.

MAKING OF THE SAUCE:

1. First it starts with sugar! *A whole fucking lot!* The most prominent ingredient in the Pad Thai will actually be the sugar. Don't freak out like some screaming banshee…sugar this, sugar that, asdflkjeioeshhs SUGAR IS THE WORST THING EVER!!!! When divided amongst how many meals this makes, it is probably less sugar than a soft drink. Many of the people who complain about cooking with sugar in the food want me to make BAKING videos of sweets…go figure. [end rant]

   You can use either a vegan white sugar or turbinado sugar. It will come out more orange in the end with white sugar and more brownish with turbinado. It is difficult to see the sugar in the picture because it is underlying the other ingredients. There is a bit more sugar than both of the other ingredients in this picture combined. The next most abundant ingredient is crushed peanuts, which you created in a bloodied frenzy above. Finally, you need either a tamarind soup base powder or tamarind paste. In the picture I am using a tamarind soup base powder. It looks like brown sugar here with large "boulders" of soup base. You will find two types of tamarind paste in many Asian stores. One comes in a large block of solid blackish tamarind paste. The other will be a jar of liquidy brown sludge. Go for the sludge. Though it looks like it came out of an anus, it will blend in better and be easier to use in general.

You will need a good bit of tamarind paste or soup base, but less than the sugar and just less than or equal to the peanuts. Picture 1A shows the same step but with tamarind paste. This will give you an idea on how much of the tamarind sludge to use.

2. In this step, I have added a bit of water, a few knife tips of peanut butter (this helps give it a more peanutty taste), a few good squirts of sriracha, and grated a few cloves of fresh garlic in. Don't be afraid of plenty of sriracha. Even though it looks it, it won't be that hot and it will give the dish an awesome overall color in the end. Remember the pure unmanifest blandness of the rice noodles. Also in this step you will give the mixture a small pour of vinegar, just 2 or 3 quick pours will be plenty.

3. Mix this up well and add a handful of cilantro. How much is a handful? Make a black metal claw with your hand by raising it in victory with fingers spread. Then take cilantro in your hand and shake it a bit just to show your power. What is left is a handful.

4. Now the actual cooking shall begin. Summon your flames upon some oil in a pan (either canola, peanut, or coconut oil). Place your cut-up tomatoes and stalks of green onion in your pan. Stir around till the tomatoes are slightly cooked down. Only a few minutes should suffice. While this is going on, heat up your deep fryer and prepare to scald your pressed tofu. Fry the tofu just till lightly brown. Too long will leave you gnawing at the hardened flesh of plant hide.

5. Add in your mung bean sprouts saving a precious few aside for the end to mix in some raw sprouts.

TAMARIND PASTE
(AKA TAMARIND CONCENTRATE)

This can be found in Indian or Asian grocery stores, and will come in two main forms: a solid block that is semi-soft, or a liquid container (a jar of fairly liquidy brownish stuff). Either will ultimately work for making shit; however, you want the liquid container. The liquid container mixes far better with your dish in general. The solid block is kind of a pain to get mixed in well and will have hard seeds to remove that suck.

*The company in this picture does not endorse this book or the Vegan Black Metal Chef project.

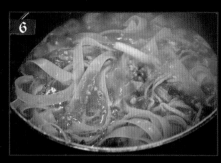

6. Before engaging in this critical action, turn your heat up as high as it can go. When the pot or pan has increased sufficiently in heat, add your drained, softened rice noodles and pour in your sauce. The goal is to evaporate the water out as fast as the beast can corrupt a feeble mind.

7. Add in your fried tofu chunks and stir this mixture with all your might. You must keep stirring with a fury while the water evaporates. With a pot or pan steeped in such fires of hell, you must continue to stir so the dark ones do not take the bottom of your dish. As the final amounts of water leave this plane of existence, the noodles will fry a bit in the oily remains. When all water has been expunged and the noodles lightly fried, quickly transfer to a spiked serving dish. Cast the spell of more crushed peanuts on the top of your summoning.

Your work in this creation is complete!

RICE OF THE REALM (ASIAN)

There are many, many Asian types of rice. Go to the Asian store and you will be bewildered with the choices and selection. I shall narrow this down to one essential and one optional. The essential is jasmine rice. This shit is so flavorful and versatile, it can be used for each and every dish in this section. The optional is sushi rice. This can be used as a general rice beyond just its use in sushi, but sushi can also be made fantastically well with jasmine rice. There are many other types of rices in the Asian store. Give them a try. See what you think. Sadly, the brand actually matters with rice. Try a few different brands of the same rice. Decide on which ones you like. You will be surprised at how different various brands of the same rice taste.

*The company in this picture does not endorse this book or the Vegan Black Metal Chef project.

FRIED RICE

Fried Rice Palace

SPELL REAGENTS (INGREDIENTS)

- **Jasmine or calrose rice** *(made fresh or a day or two old in the refrigerator)*
- **White pepper**
- **Vegetable broth**
- **Soy sauce**
- **Sesame oil**
- **Chili powder or chili oil** *(optional)*
- **Garlic or garlic powder**
- **Ginger** *(optional)*
- **Any other Asian spices or premade sauce you want**

- **Various vegetables and/or vegan meats** *(anything you want in the fried rice)*
- **Cooking oil** *(any besides olive oil)*

Fried rice is easy as fuck. Yet the dark gods decree: it is easy to fuck up. The methods separate the chosen from the fallen. CONTINUED

Hear the cries from the fried rice palace! Listen, ghouls: the concept here is to make the sauce separately from the sautéing vegetables. Then, in the final moment, when all is combined, we call upon the fires of hell to seal the creation.

Begin with heating and mixing the vegetable broth, soy sauce, sesame oil, garlic, chili powder, and any other Asian spices or mixes you desire. This will undergo unholy metamorphosis in the sauce pot as it boils.

One spice from among the victors shall stand out in the flavor palate.

This is white pepper. It is the key to life here. Add a bit of it. Don't go fucking crazy; you can add more in the end.*

Sauté some vegetables and any vegan meats in the dark splendor of your cooking oil.

Now the critical step! Turn your heat up to high and invoke the flames of wrath.

Call upon the rice and some sauce into this dish. Do not saturate the rice with sauce. Better that the unholy spirits see the waste of extra sauce, than the use of too much.

Stir your creation! When it looks glorious and done, justice shall appear before you!

*The company in this picture does not endorse this book or the Vegan Black Metal Chef project.

DON'T FIGHT FOR YOUR LIMITATIONS

In one of my favorite books, *Illusions* by Richard Bach, there is the line: "Fight for your limitations and sure enough, they are yours." Do you have a problem for every solution? Is there no way anything can go in your favor? Whenever there is the chance that things can go well…do you sabotage that chance? Oftentimes people fight hard to remain in their place in life, instead of facing changes head on to grow. It can be comfortable to stay with the situation you know as opposed to changing your behavior. To me this is another form of not taking responsibilty for one's actions. Blaming the outside instead of looking within, accepting what is, and seizing your power to do something about a situation. Next time, you are arguing with yourself or others about why your life can or can not change…don't worry, either way you will be right.

TEMPURA VEGETABLES

At the Heart of Tempura

SPELL REAGENTS (INGREDIENTS)

- **Various vegetables** *(I like broccoli, sweet potato, Japanese sweet potato, onion, carrots, bell pepper, tofu, seitan, etc.)*
- **Tempura batter**

- **Carbonated water** *(unflavored)*
- **Canola, peanut, or other neutral oil for deep frying**

Japanese tempura is the art of the light crisp fry batter. The secret to a correct summoning relies on one major thing: very cold carbonated water. In preparation for this rite, I place the bottle of soda water into the depths of the freezer for 10-15 minutes. It will get cold and just a bit like the icy peaks of the North, but not like the frozen Arctic.

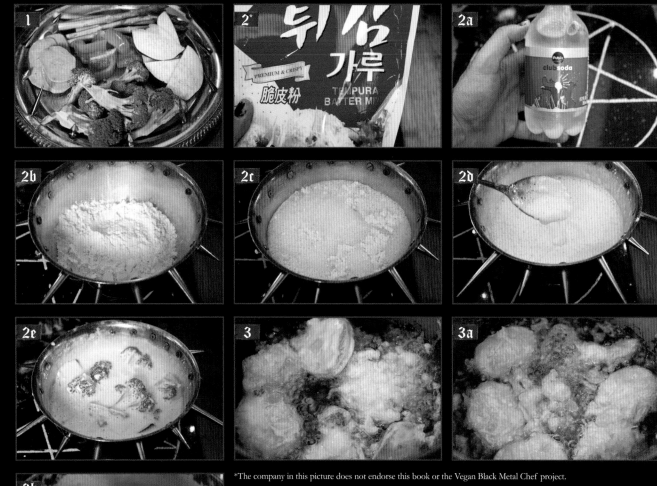

*The company in this picture does not endorse this book or the Vegan Black Metal Chef project.

Special tempura batter can be purchased from the Asian store. You can make your own, but it is cheap enough to just get this premade for perfection.

The only other aspect to keep in mind is that you will not be frying each sacrifice for long. This means that you must cut potatoes very thin. Each should not be the width of many knife-blades.

1. Cut some vegetables upon the altar of Satan.

2. Summon forth your tempura batter and cold carbonated water. Pour some tempura batter in your summoning bowl and add enough soda water to make a semi-thin batter paste. Plunge some vegetables into the quagmire of this batter.

3. Deep fry the vegetables only until the outside is crisp and perfect. Different ones will turn different colors. They should not have their souls fried out of them.

Serve with your favorite Asian dipping sauce. Soy sauce mixed with wasabi paste hits the dark spot within.

DEEP FRYER

An incredibly useful tool throughout this text will be the deep fryer. As an alternative, you can always fill a large pot partially up with oil and heat it up on the stove; however, for around twenty dollars, you will get tremendous value for your money.

Deep fried food does not use as much oil as you would think. The water in the food turns to steam and repels the oil outward. Pan frying often uses far more oil and in a much less controlled way. You do not need to change the oil every time.

THE MYSTERY OF FIRE AND WATER

A Bulgarian Mystic named Omram Mikeal Ivanov wrote an incredible book called *The Mystery Of Fire And Water*. One of its main premises is that, like a metallurgist, we shape ourselves in the metaphorical fire. To enter the fires, we rise to the heights of mind: philosophical questioning, meditative contemplation, and insight. This is the fire that shapes our ideas. They are pounded with the hammers of the mind into the best set of actions your mind can craft. Yet this is not enough. Just as with the analogy of the blacksmith, it must then be plunged into the hardening waters. The waters are life: trial, tribulation, action and consequence. Only then can you see if your actions, world view, or thought patterns are not beneficial to you. Go into the fires and waters and reshape yourself until you are happy with the result. We are always reshapeable if you are willing to do the work.

PEANUT SAUCE

SPELL REAGENTS (INGREDIENTS)

- **Crushed peanuts** *(optional)*
- **Peanut butter**
- **Coconut milk** *(or water)*
- **Hoisin sauce**
- **Sugar**
- **Garlic powder**
- **Sesame oil**

Peanut sauce is whispered in legend among the ancients. Its glory extends throughout every plane of existence. Once this has entered your life, you will quickly make so much that you shall become sick with demonic possession. Even the vomit will taste good. Then after a period of rest, your mind and stomach will learn temperance…maybe.

Peanut Sauce and Her Embrace

1. This incantation starts with some peanut butter. How much? However the fuck much you want. Have you learned nothing?

2. Pour the coconut milk like angels' blood around the peanut butter and stir until the magic alchemy happens. The peanut butter will merge creating a smooth creamy beige mixture. Where there once were two, there is now a decadent one.

3. Vomit a glob of hoisin sauce into this crucible. Adjust the hoisin amount for additional richness and depth.

4. Finish this by mixing in some sugar, a bit of garlic powder, and a drizzle of sesame oil.

The blinding light of infinite existence may shine forth from it.

VEGETABLE BROTH

Vegetable broth is a key ingredient in many of these dishes. It is one of the secrets of ultimate flavor and satisfaction. It is critical that you get at least one good vegetable broth, and preferably a variety of them. Here is where experimentation comes in. No one can know every vegetable broth in every country, so go to the store, get every one you see and try them throughout the week. Some will be good, some not so much. There are many types to choose from in the Asian store. Look for an entire aisle or section of various broth bouillon cubes. Many of these will be vegan. Read the ingredients and try several. If a store has an entire section of something, they probably use it. In the Asian store there is also an MSG-free vegetable broth substitute called "vegetarian seasoning" or "mushroom vegetarian essence." This tastes fantastic and should be included in the variety of shit you get. You just take a small handful of this powder and add it to water.

SUMMER ROLLS

SPELL REAGENTS (INGREDIENTS)

- Spring roll wrappers *(rice paper)*
- Lettuce
- Tofu
- Cornstarch *(optional)*
- Fresh basil
- Fresh mint *(optional)*
- Fried red onion pieces
- Fried garlic pieces *(optional)*
- Rice noodles

All rolls have a season, yet only the spring and summer rolls are worth a damn. The fall roll just had a bunch of decaying leaves, and the winter roll is just ice, spikes, and woods. The winter roll is the most metal, even if it's inedible.

Summer rolls are unique in how much they resemble condom rolls. Served soft and fresh like a virgin sacrifice, they are bathed in the juice of peanut sauce, and splashed with the blood of sriracha.

The company in this picture does not endorse this book or the Vegan Black Metal Chef project.

The Burning Shadows of Summer Rolls

It begins now...

Have a pot, pan, or large bowl with water to submerge the summer roll wrappers. Also have an altar of sacrifice to put the wet wrapper and make the roll. Prepare some fried tofu with a cornstarch batter as declared on high in the Vegan Meat section (page 196). Summon the peanut sauce from the previous page. Peanut sauce is the life blood of the summer roll.

Let the feast of rolls begin:

1. Boil some thin rice noodles for mere minutes, such that you have a mat of banshee hair.

2. Once all of the above ingredients have been gathered together, plunge and drown a summer roll wrapper in water (any temperature) for 5 seconds. After this round of torture, lay it on its place of final rest, ready to be stuffed and wrapped.

3. In this mystic set of ingredients, there are a few to look for in the markets of the East. Picture 3 shows fried red onion. There are several items similar to this which include fried garlic, and fried shallot.

4. The fresh mint and fried garlic are optional, but get them. While the peanut sauce carries most of the flavor, these add a great addition to the basil and fried red onion. Place all of the filling ingredients of the summer roll upon the wet wrapper and stare at its majesty.

5. Roll this glorious perfection up and tuck in the sides as it rolls. Four or five of these make a meal in itself. Dip in your copious amounts of peanut sauce and top with crushed peanuts. Serve with utter satisfaction.

RAMEN STIR FRY

SPELL REAGENTS (INGREDIENTS)

- **Ramen noodles** *(or any noodles)*
- **Small variety of vegetables** *(ex. green onion, mushrooms, bell peppers, snow pea...*
- **Vegetable broth**
- **Soy sauce**
- **Optional hoisin sauce, or other vegan premade stir fry sauce or oyster sauce**
- **Tofu or seitan** *(optional)*
- **Other spices: Chopped garlic, chopped ginger, sesame oil, chili powder or oil**
- **Sugar** *(optional)*
- **Fried garlic bits** *(optional)*
- **Fried shallots** *(optional)*
- **Cooking oil** *(ex. canola oil, coconut oil, other vegetable oil, **NOT** olive oil)*

Dark Noodle Stirfry Divine

The number of the pots for this dish shall be three. Never one or two, but three. Five is right out. A large pot for boiling the noodles, a smaller pot for making the sauce, and a large pan or wok where the ultimate conjuring takes place.

Cut up a small variety of vegetables. Keep in mind that your goal is not to eat one of everything in existence. This will not be the only meal you ever make. And even if it is your last, it will still be better if you don't put every vegetable in the grocery store into it. Either way, choose between three to five vegetables you want to include in your stir fry.

Prepare your three pots for this ritual. Start some water heating in the pot for boiling your noodles, and heat some oil in your large pan or wok.

Ramen noodles just make you feel like you are winning the war of food costs. There are many types of cheap noodles, but this one is somehow crazy cheap.

First prepare the sauce.

1. Get some vegetable broth or a vegetable soup cube and some water. Seriously people, you can use regular vegetable broth and it will come out fine…however, for total world domination, you should go to the Asian store and get some Asian vegetable broth. There will be a few different spices in these that will complete your life, bring you happiness, and make you rich (not exactly). It will taste more "Asian." In the picture, the floating brown bits are little pieces of fried garlic. This is also available at the Asian store. They are pretty intense so a little goes a long way.

2. Add some soy sauce, sesame oil, grated garlic, grated ginger and optionally some of the additional hoisin sauce or other premade stir fry sauces. Now that you know the concept, you can experiment around with all sorts of shit. Remember that you do not need to combine everything in manifested existence together.

3. Bring this all to a boil and reduce the heat to a medium hell.

CONTINUED

Make the stir fry.

4. If seitan is desired in this ritual, you must appease the dark one by browning it thoroughly first. This step is of utmost importance. I will repeat these words every time until the gods can be summoned with proper respect. The number one reason for terrible-tasting seitan is not cooking it enough first. It should look well browned all around.

5. After the seitan is pleased, sauté the vegetables you've chosen by adding them to the pan with the seitan. In this case I used red cabbage, green onion, and red and yellow bell peppers.

6. At this point, boil the noodles for about 2-3 minutes, taking them off the heat a minute or so before they are fully very soft. The noodles will have a better consistency if they "finish" cooking in the sauce.

7. When the vegetables are crisp yet cooked to your desired state, add the heated sauce and dump in the (drained) noodles. Turn the heat up to near high and scald them all for 2–3 more minutes until all of the sauce is absorbed.

8. Top it off with some cashews or peanuts if the devil beckons you to do so.

The result of the ritual should look something like this: ▶

KUNG POW CHICKUN

One Road To Kung Pow Bay

SPELL REAGENTS (INGREDIENTS)

- **Chickun-style seitan** *(or any vegan meat)*
- **Various vegetables** *(pick a few)*
- **Peanuts**
- **Jasmine or other Asian rice**
- **Asian black vinegar** *(zhenjiang vinegar)*
- **Soy sauce**
- **Vegetable broth**
- **Árbol chilies**
- **Sugar**
- **Garlic**
- **Ginger**
- **Cooking oil** *(canola, peanut, vegetable, safflower, coconut, etc...anything but olive oil)*

The dark art of American Chinese takeout is revealed before your eyes throughout this section. This rite requires one weird ingredient: vinegar as black as your heart must be purchased at the Asian store. Do not neglect this step, as it is the dark core of this dish. The other ingredient you must quest for are the árbol chilies. These can be found either in the Asian store or in the Hispanic aisle of many grocery stores. One bag is cheap and lasts a long time. Get them for maximum satisfaction.

Preparation: At some point in this ritual, deep fry some vegan meat in the same batter as the Grim and Frostbitten Cauliflower (page 118). Do not use curry powder in the batter.

1. This begins in the traditional way with the preparation of the sauce. Grate some garlic and ginger into a pot along with some sugar. Gaze upon this first, as it is difficult to see amidst the seas of liquid to follow.

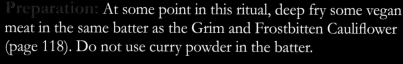

2. This is how the vinegar appears in this mortal world.*

3. The vegetable broth is life. Of course you have quested long and hard, fought many daemons and monsters for a good vegetable broth. Use either a liquid broth or a soup cube and water.

4. At this time, the blackened flood of soy sauce will be poured in, as seen on the right.

5. Add the árbol chilies and bring this spicy potion to a boil. Reduce the heat, and slowly boil into a thickening bile until everything else is done.

6. Sauté with haste some vegetables in your cooking oil. They quickly become turgid and ready.

7. By this time, you have cast out many spirits of water in your sauce. It has thickened and become worthy.

8. The fried chickun pieces are glorious…add them. The kung pow sauce yearns for battle; send it forth. Have a handful of peanuts attack from above.

*The company in this picture does not endorse this book or the Vegan Black Metal Chef project.

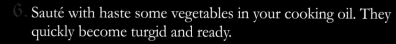

The final moment looks as such. ▼

CONSCIOUSNESS IS LIFE

It's all about bringing consciousness to your life and actions. That is it. With consciousness, we are truly alive. Consciousness is not an on and off condition; it is a continuum with varying degrees. We are always conscious to a degree and unconscious to a degree. The more conscious we are, the more choices we have. If we are living in deep unconsciousness, things always seem to "happen to us." The world becomes very difficult to deal with. The more consciousness we bring to our lives, the more responsibility we take for our actions, and the more we will actually get to choose to live how we wish. It can be difficult at first, especially if you have been living in greater unconsciousness up to this point. Doing this can be a bitter pill to swallow. It is the choice of the Matrix. Do you take the pill that wakes you up into temporary pain, or the pill that puts you back to sleep in a world that feels comfortable but out of your control? Take the path of consciousness, it is well worth it.

ASIAN GREEN BEANS

SPELL REAGENTS (INGREDIENTS)

- **Vegetable broth**
- **Fresh green beans** *(or pole beans)*
- **Rice noodles**
- **Soy sauce**
- **Sugar**
- **Garlic**
- **Mushrooms** *(any type)*
- **Onions**
- **Bell peppers** *(optional)*
- **Hoisin sauce**
- **Sesame oil** *(optional)*
- **Any other premade stir fry sauce** *(optional)*
- **Cashews, mixed nut blend, or peanut**
- **Cooking oil** (anything but olive oil)

Once again, the familiar tale of Asian cooking, always and forever, three pots will be needed in this unholy communion: one for the sauce, one for the noodles, and one pot to rule them all! It goes without saying that one should start heating your pot of water for the noodles in the beginning. Only a fool would waste a picture space on such things!

Withstand the Fall of Asian Green Beans

1. Begin this journey with some vegetable broth, or a vegetable broth soup cube in some water.

2. While upon a high heat hellfire, add some soy sauce, a bit of sugar, grate in a few cloves of garlic, give a squirt or two of hoisin sauce, and optionally add a small amount of sesame oil, other stir-fry sauce or vegan oyster sauce. Heat this up to a boil, then reduce the heat to a steady medium slow bubble.

3. Sauté the green beans first. If you use canned green beans, I will appear before you only to kick you in the taint. Canned green beans taste as if there was a large man at the cannery who puts each of the green beans in his mouth and sucks out the flavor before spitting them into the can. Use fresh green beans and sauté them in the oil for a few minutes.

4. While the green beans are not yet fully cooked, add the onions and mushrooms and proceed to stir like a whirling dervish in ecstasy. Stir in and sauté the whole of this creation. The point of this is not to sauté everything to death, but merely cook these reagents such that they are no longer raw. They should be crisp and not a shriveled mess upon completion.

5. When the sacred balance of crispiness and cooked-ness has reached its teetering balance, add in your sauce and cook for one more minute. Remove from the hellfires and dole some of the green bean and sauce mixture out upon your boiled and drained rice noodles.

Finish this incantation with the liberal application of either cashews, mixed nuts, or peanuts. This step is not optional. It is the majestic blend of the green bean awesomeness and the nuts that create a flavor explosion not usually allowed among mortal men.

BANH MI

SPELL REAGENTS (INGREDIENTS)

- **Tofu** *(or seitan, or whatever)*
- **Carrot**
- **Daikon radish** *(or any radish)*
- **Cilantro**
- **Cucumber**
- **French bread**
- **Salt**
- **Sugar**
- **Vinegar**

OPTIONAL ADDITIONS

- **Jalapeño slices**
- **Tomato**
- **Avocado**
- **Fried red onion**
- **Fried garlic**
- **Vegan mayonnaise**

- **Sriracha**
- **Vegetable broth**
- **Sesame oil**
- **Other awesome sandwich shit...**

One of the great wonders of this universe: the unexpected perfection of the Vietnamese sub. What unholy alchemy could have crafted such flavors together?

Incredibly easy to make, yet it carries a curse…there is preparation involved.

The dark gods are merciful to the wicked; there are only about 5–7 minutes of work. Yet it takes half a day to overnight to complete its transformation.

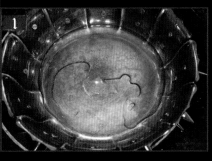

Banh Mi Fire Death

If French bread hath been purchased, you are going to want banh mi sandwiches. The moment the bread manifests itself into your thought or existence, Begin The Preparation Ritual!!!

Invoke the magic of salt, sugar, vinegar, and water.

1. Produce two pours of vinegar upon your summoning bowl. Similar to the ritual for sushi rice or rice balls, mix the sugar (brownish in the picture), salt, vinegar, and water together for a perfect pickling liquid. The exact amount matters not!!! Just get some fucking salt, sugar and vinegar in there. Eyeball that shit. Done.

2. Cut some cucumber into stalks. Take an enchanted war blade (or potato peeler) and peel some thin carrot, and daikon radish strips. Mix them into your pickling liquid until fully submerged into the depths. Place the covered container in the chilled hell of your refrigerator for at least half a day or overnight.

3. Summon forth some fried tofu with cornstarch batter as directed in the Vegan Meats section (page 196).

   Optionally, to make the earth shake with taste, heat a small amount of vegetable broth with sesame oil and toss the cornstarch fried tofu in.

   Toast your French bread sandwich sarcophagus. Place your tofu, cucumber, daikon radish and carrot slices in. Top with heaps of cilantro, salt, pepper, and jalapeño slices.

   Top this shit with whatever you want. These are the basics of an amazing banh mi sandwich.

Many variations spew from this archetype.

THAI CURRIES

SPELL REAGENTS (INGREDIENTS)

- **Thai curry paste** *(small can — you can use larger ones, but only a very small amount is needed)*
- **Coconut milk** *(highest calories and fat can you can find)*
- **Tofu** *(or seitan, or whatever vegan protein)*
- **Various vegetables** *(good choices include any 3 or 4 of the following: potato, celery, onions, carrot, bell pepper, bamboo shoots, water chestnut, broccoli, green beans, mushrooms)*

- **Salt**
- **Sugar**
- **Chili powder**
- **Garlic powder**
- **Peanut butter** *(optional)*
- **Peanuts** *(optional)*
- **Jasmine rice** *(white or brown)*

The mystic land of Thailand has long been known for its array of food fit for the gods. Among its myriad of deathly perfections are the unique Thai curries. To make fresh, you would need difficult-to-find spell reagents in mysterious quantities. Luckily for the dark side, cheating yields the best results possible!

74

Thai Curry Doctrine

◀ 1. This is a can of coconut milk. Many are like it, yet they are not equal.

Your goal is to purchase the one with the most calories and fat. Do not be deceived by the mere number. One must multiply this by the servings in the can to divulge the truth.

◀ This is a can of Thai curry paste. Read the ingredients with care, for not all are vegan.

2. Start by heating a small amount of coconut milk in a pot. Add half the can of curry paste to the heated milk and fry until fragrant. CONTINUED

*The companies in these pictures do not endorse this book or the Vegan Black Metal Chef project.

ASLEEP OR AWAKE

When we become our thoughts, we are asleep. When we observe our thoughts, we are awake. When asleep, if our thoughts are attacked, we are attacked. If our thoughts are broken, we are broken. When awake, our thoughts are free to come and go, to be accepted and discarded as they are needed. When we are our thoughts, we justify insanity because we need to justify our actions. When we observe our thoughts, we see thoughts that are undesirable. We either change or wait for the time when we can change. When we are our thoughts, there is separation. There is us and them. There is constant fear because the ego is pure separation. It lives of off thoughts of us and them. When we observe our thoughts, there are no barriers, because we just are. When we are our thoughts, we swirl from the past and future, between depression and anxiety. We are at a race toward death. We can not truly enjoy any journey because we are never present. We are always somewhere else. When we observe our thoughts, we recognize depression, anxiety—every feeling that comes up. When we observe our thoughts we recognize all feelings good and bad. We are present for all of them and present in life.

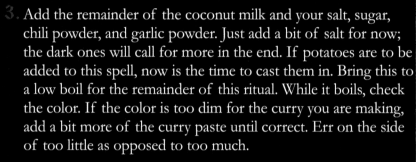

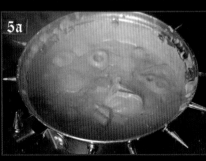

3. Add the remainder of the coconut milk and your salt, sugar, chili powder, and garlic powder. Just add a bit of salt for now; the dark ones will call for more in the end. If potatoes are to be added to this spell, now is the time to cast them in. Bring this to a low boil for the remainder of this ritual. While it boils, check the color. If the color is too dim for the curry you are making, add a bit more of the curry paste until correct. Err on the side of too little as opposed to too much.

4. You have cut some tofu into small squares, pressed the water out as is written in the book of tofu (in the Vegan Meats section on page 194). Brown the tofu well on both sides. When the tofu hast reached browning perfection, toss in your vegetables. Sauté all with the fury of the gods.

5. By now, the potatoes are done! They should be easily pierced with the mystical knife. If the curry is crazy thick, you may thin it with water, yet it should be perfect! Add peanut butter to make it peanut curry.

6. Pour the curry over the vegetables and conjoin upon a plate of jasmine white or brown rice.

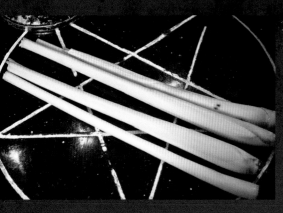

LEMONGRASS

This is lemongrass. You will usually find it in Asian stores. Do not buy the frozen or powdered forms; they are useless. Buy the fresh stalks, and cut to make thin circles down the entire length (like a green onion). You can then just add them to the broth you are making. The taste is seriously fucking amazing and somewhat unexpected. Do this.

FOCUS ON WHAT YOU ARE FOR

People think veganism is just being against things. One side of the coin is to be against the exploitation of animals. It can also be for eating plant-based foods and products with no animal products or exploitation. If you are against something, you are in a state of struggle. If you are for something, you are in a state of enjoyment. It is far more sustainable to continuously be in a state of enjoyment and excitement than a state of struggle. Struggle is draining. No one can stay in struggle forever.

I enjoy finding a large variety of plant-based things to eat. There are so damn many I have not even tried them all yet! I enjoy bringing consciousness to my actions so I can at least know the consequences of my actions.

Veganism does not make you perfect. Struggling against things can make you feel "better than" what you are struggling against. Don't fall into this trap. It is the trap of the ego, the self that feels separate from the world and likes to emphasize its separateness.

Focus on what you are "for" most of the time and see the world light up within you and around you.

SPELL REAGENTS (INGREDIENTS)

- Sushi rice or jasmine rice
- Salt
- Sugar
- Vinegar
- Wasabi

SUSHI FILLING

- Asparagus
- Carrots
- Cucumber
- Avocado
- Spinach

- Mushrooms
- Sweet potato
- Cashews

LOTS OF SHIT, MANY EXAMPLES TO FOLLOW.

NORI (SEAWEED)

When looking around in the Asian store to make sushi or rice balls you will find two main types of nori: seasoned nori or unseasoned nori. The seasoned always comes in some kind of foil or metallic package and has spices and sesame (or other) oil in the ingredients. The unseasoned comes in either a foil or non-foil package and has only one ingredient: seaweed.

I typically use the seasoned for rice balls and the unseasoned for sushi. You can use either in soups by breaking them into small pieces and dropping into any Asian soup.

Within Sushi I Burn

Rice Preparation

1. The secret to the truly demonic flavor of sushi rice lies in three spell reagents…salt, sugar, and vinegar. In the enchanted pot you shall see about how much sugar and salt the spirits use for one cup of rice and two cups of water. The sugar is brown in this picture since it is of the turbinado kind. Use whatever sugar you wish to sacrifice.

2. Follow this magic formula for the jasmine or sushi rice: the ancient alchemists once said, "Use twice as much water as rice." These were truly wise mystics, as the formula will yield perfection, even to this day. After adding the water and rice, give the entire compound a quick pour or two of vinegar. Some people flip out and worry endlessly about the type of vinegar. Just get some plain-ass white vinegar in there.

   Bring to a boil, reduce heat to low. The rice is summoned to this realm when all water is absorbed.

   Remove from the heat and pour into a sacred bowl. You can let it cool, but that takes too fucking long…just keep going.

Before we get into 100,000 types of different sushi… you must learn the ancient rolling ways.

3. Prepare your bamboo mat upon your altar of sacrifice. Lay the nori sheet upon it in the traditional way. Wet your hands and cast the spell of dampness upon the nori by lightly rubbing your moist hands on its surface. Spread a thin layer of sushi rice atop the nori by any means necessary.

4. Fill with the various innards of your sacrifice. On the next page you shall find much inspiration. CONTINUED

5. Begin the rolling process by curling the rice and nori over your layer of innards. This is where you have to stop, and while keeping the nori rolled over the filling, pull the bit of bamboo mat from under your finger back so you can roll the rest of it. Proceed to finish rolling the sushi in the normal way that makes sense. This is not difficult…. just try it and make it happen.

Don't complicate shit. These pages shall plant the seed of inspiration within your dark mind.

PANKO ENCRUSTED ASPARAGUS WITH RED BELL PEPPER AND GREEN ONION ROLL

SEAWEED SALAD ROLL

BANH MI ROLL

Pickled Daikon, Pickled Carrot, Pickled Cucumber, Fried Tofu, Jalapeño

SWEET POTATO CASHEW ROLL

Fried Sweet Potato, Cashews, Avocado or Vegan Cream Cheese

ROASTED GARLIC, FRIED SEITAN, & CARAMELIZED ONIONS ROLL

I'm not going to write that again…just try it.

RICE BALLS

SPELL REAGENTS (INGREDIENTS)

- Jasmine rice, sushi rice, or any other more sticky rice. Asian store rice.
- White vinegar or rice wine vinegar
- Sugar
- Salt
- Sesame oil
- Seasoned nori
- Sesame seeds
- Wasabi powder
- Soy sauce
- Nuts and vegetables *(any nuts, green onion, bell pepper, etc...optional)*

Are you craving sushi right the fuck now?

Do not feel like going through the time and hassle of making sushi? Rice balls will be your guiding light throughout this dark point of your life.

Little is better in life than hot, salty, nutty balls in your mouth.

Rice Balls of Might

For this ritual, you need sheets of dried seaweed. Instead of the plain sushi seaweed sheets, cast your eyes upon a different item in the Asian store. Usually in the same section or aisle that you would find regular sushi seaweed, you will see seaweed sealed in a metallic foil wrapping. The one that is most metal. Look closely at this, my child, for it reveals a deep mystery. Often it will say flavored with sesame oil or other oil and spices. This is roasted and flavored seaweed. This is what you want in life. This is what is best.

1. Begin this spell by boiling two cups of water for every cup of rice you are making. Prepare this water the same way as the ritual for sushi. Add in some sugar, one to three quick pours of vinegar, and salt. The brown muddiness in my example is from turbinado sugar. Use whatever sugar you want.

2. Add to this unholy water a layer of white sesame seeds.

3. Bring this to a boil.

4. Cover, reduce heat, and simmer as if your days are numbered.

5. Once the rice is cooked, pour forth copious amounts of sesame oil upon your rice manifestation. It appears as a wet brown stain in the example you see here. Spill it like the blood of a virgin upon a ritual altar. Mix the rice together to spread the sesame oil throughout.

6. In this fast example, add in your cashews, green onion, and bell pepper bits. Stir them, you fool.

Grab small handfuls of your sacred food, roll them up into small balls or however the hell you want. Wrap in pieces of your roasted seaweed.

SESAME TOFU

SPELL REAGENTS (INGREDIENTS)

- Tofu
- Panko
- **Self-rising flour** *(or all-purpose flour)*
- Garlic powder
- Sugar
- Sesame seeds
- Sesame oil
- **Vegetable broth** *(solid or liquid)*
- Hoisin sauce
- Soy sauce
- **Green chilies or chili powder** *(optional –but really good)*
- Jasmine rice
- **Various vegetables** *(whatever you want*

Turn past this recipe and die! Well, you are dying anyways, but until you have sesame tofu you have not truly lived. This dish will electrify the darkened depths of your soul with a mixture of crispy fried outside, hot soft inside, and drenched in a sweet, spicy, sesame glaze that will ignite your inner core. You might even find purpose in your meaningless existence.

This dish is really a mixture of two concepts: making panko-encrusted fried tofu and making the sweet sesame sauce. You can use both of these in many ways and in many meals. The sesame sauce is good on damn near everything. You can just put it on rice, eat it and it's awesome. The panko-encrusted tofu is an amazing fried protein to dip into every sauce of the abyss.

Progenies of the Sesame Tofu Apocalypse

The ritual for the panko-encrusted tofu is in the Vegan Meats section (page 198). The cryptic writings below detail the sauce and vegetable summoning.

Read the following words with fear and wonder:

Big fucking surprise…it starts with vegetable broth.

1. Satan likes to use a vegetable broth cube from the Asian store, along with adding some water. However, any liquid or powder broth will do. Decay your soul with copious amounts of sugar. This is going to boil down to a thin glaze, so add plenty of fucking sugar! Add a large glop of hoisin sauce. This will emphasize the abyssal thickness while adding to the satanic sweetness.

2. Add soy sauce from your black heart, garlic or garlic powder from your putrid breath, and chopped green chilies or chili powder from your fiery arse! Fresh chilies are acquired at most Asian or Indian stores and add an unnaturally awesome spicy natural taste. If you are foolish enough not to have fresh chilies, you can shamefully substitute chili powder or chili oil. Suffocate with a covering of sesame seeds. The sesame seeds should cover your pot like a mat of ants. Finally, pour forth an eyeball full of sesame oil and bring it to a boil. Reduce your heat to medium low to complete this sinister simmer. This will boil down and thicken while you make the tofu, rice and vegetables.

3. Hack up various vegetables and toss them in a pan with some oil. Sauté the vegetables for several minutes. The idea is not to cook the fuck out of them, just to get them lightly sautéed, crispy and perfect…like the dark one himself. Add a bit of the sesame sauce into this pan toward the end. Just a fucking drop! It should not looked "sauced," just a blood spatter for some flavor.

4. Cast the vegetables and tofu atop a mighty mountain of jasmine rice. Splatter liberally with your sesame glaze.

The final creation is electrifying to the soul. You will not believe its utter taste destruction!

Oracle of Inspiration

Asian Dumpling Noodle Soup

SPELL REAGENTS (INGREDIENTS)

- Vegetable broth
- Noodles
- Vegan frozen dumplings
- Green onion *(optional)*
- Seaweed pieces *(optional)*
- Sesame oil *(optional)*
- Sriracha or chili oil *(optional)*

This is simplicity itself. Boil some vegetable broth. Toss in your noodles and a few frozen dumplings. If the noodles do not cook fast…hold off on throwing in the dumplings until the last four or so minutes. Optionally, dump in some sriracha (it tastes amazing when boiled with the broth), sesame oil, sliced green onion, lemongrass, or whatever you want. In the end, you can also add a few pieces of seaweed flakes. You have bought seaweed because you are making sushi, right? If not, you are doing everything wrong in life. Add a few pieces to soup for an awesome flavor.

Singapore Noodles

SPELL REAGENTS (INGREDIENTS)

- Tofu
- Seitan *(or chickun-style seitan)*
- Vegan shrimp *(optional)*
- Vegetables
- Thin rice noodles *(preferably vermicelli, round style)*
- Vegetable broth
- Soy sauce
- Curry powder
- Sesame oil
- Garlic
- Chili oil
- Cooking oil *(anything but olive oil)*

Singapore noodles sure as hell don't come from Singapore. They are a common American Asian dish of curried rice noodles with vegan meats, vegetables, curry powder, and chili oil. The chili oil carries a good bit of the taste here so do not neglect it. Follow the same concepts as the Ramen Noodle Stirfry (page 64), adding some curry powder to your sauce pot. Boil the rice noodles separately. Deep fry or pan fry the tofu and sauté the other vegan meats, being sure to well brown any seitan. Sauté the vegetables until crisp and combine with the boiled rice noodles and the sauce. Turn the heat up to high and stir constantly to evaporate any additional liquid.

Scan for updates.

Oracle of Inspiration

Tofu Stir-Fried with Lemongrass and Chilies

SPELL REAGENTS (INGREDIENTS)

- **Tofu** *(or any vegan meat)*
- **Lemongrass** *(fresh only)*
- **Chili oil and optional fresh chilies**
- **Vegetables**
- **Jasmine rice**
- **Soy sauce**
- **Vegetable broth**
- **Garlic**
- **Sugar**
- **Sesame oil**
- **Cooking oil** *(anything but olive oil)*
- **Ginger** *(optional)*

Use the tofu concepts (page 194) to prepare and fry the tofu. Use the freezing tofu concepts for an airier texture.

Use the same concepts as the Ramen Noodle Stir-Fry (page 64) to prepare the sauce. Slice the lemongrass down its length into small circles. One stalk should be enough. If part of the stalk is ruined, use two. Add the small lemongrass slivers to the sauce pot. They will release their flavor as the sauce boils.

Stir fry the vegetables and add the fried tofu and the broth at the end. Serve over jasmine rice.

Pad See Ew

SPELL REAGENTS (INGREDIENTS)

- **Rice noodles**
- **Vegan oyster sauce** *(or stir-fry sauce)*
- **Vegetable broth**
- **Garlic or fried garlic**
- **White pepper**
- **Sugar**
- **Soy sauce**
- **Sesame oil**
- **Green chilies** *(optional)*
- **Cooking oil**
- **Some kind of vegan meat except jackfruit** *(optional)*
- **Vegetables**

Follow the same concept as the Ramen Noodle Stir-Fry (page 64). Use these ingredients for the sauce. Three pans/pots. One to boil the noodles, one for the sauce, one for the vegetables and vegan meats.

Pad See Ew is a sweet sauce, so add plenty of sugar. You can pour a bit of cooking oil over it all in the end to give it an oily smooth feel and taste.

In the final moments, turn the heat up to high as you add the noodles and stir-fry everything around.

HISPANIC & LATINO

Introduction – Hispanic & Latino

The intro to this section, along with every other intro in this book, is going to offend a lot of people. That's right, I'm going to lump all of Mexico, Central and South America, Spain, Portugal, and its various islands into one incorrect and incomplete section called "Hispanic & Latino food."

It will use horrid American generalizations…but you know what? I don't really give a damn!

This is beans and dirt taken to the next level.

And there are so many varieties of beans and dirt to choose from: black beans, red beans, garbanzo beans, pinto beans, etc…

Along with the beans, there is a vast array of brown, green, yellow, reddish, and whitish dirt with which to imbue the food with uncanny flavor.

From these lands also lives the mysterious fruit that wants to be fried: the plantain. Yes, you can even fry a fruit.

Cilantro: check! Olive oil: check! Paprika: check! Smoked paprika: check!

Processed spices with flavor enhancers: these will all quench your blood thirst.

RICE OF THE REALM (HISPANIC)

Medium grain rice. In many grocery stores in the United States, this is amongst the standard rices you will see. Again, different brands will taste different so try a few and get one with a Spanish-sounding name.

SMOKED PAPRIKA

Smoked paprika is a spice you can buy in many places now, and it's so damned incredible in these types of foods that you will realize that your life was mostly just a search for smoked paprika. One smell of it will convince you. It's particularly amazing in fajitas, adding a layer of richness and intense flavor.

QUINOA

Revelation of Quinoa

SPELL REAGENTS
(INGREDIENTS)

- Quinoa
- Vegetable broth
- Olive oil
- Salt

Quinoa is an arcane food that has the properties of both beans and rice, yet is neither. It is kinda nutty, kinda couscous-like, but otherwise is a bed for other shit. It can also be used as the primary object in a magical invocation.

1. Boil some vegetable broth and a quick pour of olive oil in the crucible pot of forging. Conjure half as much quinoa as the vegetable broth. Use a mere dabbling of salt.

2. Cover, reduce heat, and simmer… remembering the days that daemons walked freely on this plane.

The quinoa is now ready to do your bidding.

GUACAMOLE

SPELL REAGENTS (INGREDIENTS)

- Ripe avocado
- Jalapeño pepper
- Salt
- Cilantro
- Red onion
- Garlic
- Lime

PICKING A GOOD AVOCADO

Choosing a correct avocado is not difficult once you know what the gods desire. With the Hass, the queen of avocados, search for one whose outside essence (color) is quite dark. If it is too light, it is too young for the sacrifice. Next, hold it in your hand and squeeze lightly, as if you were holding the pulsing heart of your nemesis. If the avocado is slightly soft yet still a little bit firm, it is ready for your altar. If the avocado is soft—like mud after a three-day deluge—and the skin moves a lot when you squeeze it, it may be brown and disgusting. If the avocado holds firm to your every advance…if it defies all force by your noble hand and remains unmovable in any way, place it on your shelf of ripening; in a mere day or two it shall be a fit offering.

Blessings upon the Throne of Guacamole

This conjuration, more than any other in this section, requires incredible subtlety and finesse. If the reagents used are in excess, they become overpowering and foul. If the avocados chosen are too young or too old, the whole creation is a nightmarish green swamp.

1. First, make sure you have picked a fine sacrifice of an avocado. Refer to the "picking a good avocado" lesson at left. Without a fitting sacrifice, you have nothing.

   Next, cut a mere sliver of red onion from the mother onion. The size of the sliver will be determined by how much avocado you are summoning; it should be just enough so that when chopped fine and mixed, it will be just slightly visible. Invoke diced jalapeño and minced cilantro. Add a bit of minced garlic, but not too much, as it will overpower your creation.

2. This ritual completes by squeezing half of a fresh lime (per avocado) onto your pile and then topping it off with some salt. Mash everything together with a fork. Stop mashing when the gnarled flesh of the avocado is soft and desecrated. Eat with everything that exists.

LIBERATE SOME TIME

Yes, it takes time to be a vegan. You will need to actually read food labels in the grocery stores and finally find out what the hell you are ingesting. If you want to expand your cooking at home, try shit in this book. That'll take time. You will need to spend some time eating at new restaurants or trying new dishes at familiar restaurants. Time is required for all things in life that have value. Luckily, once you put forth the initial time (say, a full 15 hours over three months), everything will become second nature, and it will take **NO** time to be a vegan.

TACOS

SPELL REAGENTS (INGREDIENTS)

- **Veggie burger or crumbles**
- **Either premade taco spice blends, a variety of other spice blends or most of the following spices:**
  Garlic powder, pepper, cayenne pepper, chili powder, adobo, cumin
- **Soy sauce** *(or salt)*

- **Cilantro** *(optional)*
- **Cooking oil** *(either olive, canola, or whatever)*
- **Hard or soft taco shells**
- **Lettuce, tomato, onion, green onion, etc...whatever you want to top it wit**

Subterranean Taco Initiation

Throughout all time, throughout all space, there is one simple food which has reigned supreme: the taco stands alone in triumphant victory. The mixture of damn near any Mexican-tasting things either wrapped up in the soft flesh of a tortilla, or between the crisp exoskeleton of a crunchy taco shell. Ever delicious, ever simple, often messy like an impromptu assassination.

The bastardized American taco, though not traditional, is still highly addictive. One important note on tradition…

Fuck tradition. This dark art begins with the making of a "meaty" taco filling.

1. Start by heating a good bit of your cooking oil in your ritualistic pan on a medium heat. You are going to thoroughly brown your burgers/crumbles. You want to get them well browned before you break the burgers up. Browning them at this stage will guarantee the perfect texture for later on.

2. In this next step you shall pour copious amounts of spices upon your browned bits. You should spice them until they look well spiced. Here you have a lot of options. There are many ways to achieve the demonic approval of taco perfection. Even a premade store-bought taco seasoning is fair game. You can try a few and look at the ingredients to see what you like and what inspires you. The next tier of simplicity is to combine a few different spice blends. Ultimately, you can also use a combination of the individual spices listed above. The exact quantity is not so important; just make them look spiced.

At the final moment of this step, with the tempered judgment of the hand of fate, add 2-3 quick small pours of soy sauce. Imagine you are adding black salt to this grotesque mixture. Only just slightly blacken some of it, do not make it into Asian food. CONTINUED

3. At this devilish junction, the picture on this page may differ from your infernal reality. Some brands of vegan burgers/crumbles will soak up the oil and soy sauce, whereas others will remain wet-looking. If things look as dry as the Sahara Desert, you must add a fair amount of water. If you add too much, worry not…simply increase the heat of your hellish pan to have it boil off faster. It will not affect your meal.

If things look wet already, use your judgment to add a small amount of water. Add a small amount no matter what, to even out the distribution of soy sauce and spices. This will evaporate and be absorbed soon anyway. Taco filling is often somewhat wet like a slightly decayed corpse.

4. As the pieces soften further, break them up and boil away the water. This act of defiance against the gods of tradition is almost complete. Cut up your lettuce, cilantro, tomatoes and other optional toppings. Warm your taco shells in the oven of eternity and prepare your feast.

Pro Tip: The wisest cultists of seitan pour their favorite salad dressing upon their tacos for fullest enjoyment.

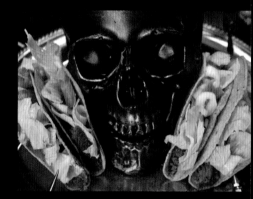

SEASONING BLENDS

Most cookbooks focus on using nothing pre-made and not having any pre-mixed seasoning. In the real world, there are tons of great pre-made blends and seasonings. One of the most versatile is the standard Italian seasoning blend. It would be a waste of time and money to buy all of the individual components when the blend is good. Search out various spice blends. Most are one to four dollars. Many are good. They will simplify and add variety to your life.

*The companies in this picture do not endorse this book or the Vegan Black Metal Chef project.

PLANTAINS

A Plantain in Rapture

1. Green plantains: Cut each plantain into 1½ -inch or so sections and remove the outside peel. Drop the sections into a bubbling oil from hell (deep fryer, ideally) and let them get a little golden brown. Then take them out with a slotted spoon of death, and place them on a ritual smashing surface. Take the bottom of a glass or your unholy mace and smash each section to flatten.

2. Place the pieces back into the oils of hell; fry again until golden brown…because frying once just isn't enough. Remove and drain on a paper towel; add salt. These go great with basically everything in this chapter, from beans to fajitas. I like to scoop whatever I'm eating on top of them, so they become something of a medieval food-soaked mini plate. Put some black beans, yellow rice and guac on top of one and taste the glory.

3. If you are lazy, plantains are available frozen and pre-fried, so warm them up, and satiate the desire within. No excuses.

For those of you who are ignorant fools, plantains are like giant bananas that taste terrible unless you boil or fry them. Sacrifice them when they are green and make a more salty, "potato-like" type of fried plantain, or you can wait until they turn black as midnight, black as pitch… and make a sweet plantain.

MADUROS

SPELL REAGENTS (INGREDIENTS)

- Ripe yellow & black plantains
- Cooking oil
- Salt

Plantain, the mystic fruit that wants to be fried, has a dark secret. Its unripe version is destined to be deep fried or pan fried over a higher heat, while the ripe sweet version needs its soul coaxed out of it slowly using gentler methods.

Enscrolled by Maduros

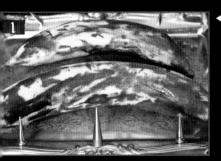

1. This is a ripe plantain. Make sure its outward essence is blackened or at least partially so.

   Skin their bodies until a naked husk remains. Cut this into semi-thin slices. You shall imagine them to be three quarters in the oil and one quarter out. Cut them to the size you think shall fulfill those wishes.

2. Heat your oil on medium low. When the fire daemons have sufficiently licked your oil, place the plantains in. They should bubble like the witch's cauldron on a slow boil.

   In the infernal alchemy of the pan, the sugars in the fruit begin to caramelize. Their inner darkness begins to slowly emerge.

   When this occurs, flip them within the oil.

   Use magic tongs of flipping or whatever way you can, get them to turn over and brown the other side.

   Continue to flip them until they look like golden glazed gods.

3. Place upon a paper towel to soak the excess fat.

   The leftover oil shall go into your deep fryer of the ancients.

   Serve with everything, every day.

MOFONGO

SPELL REAGENTS (INGREDIENTS)

- **Green plantains**
- **Fresh garlic**
- **Olive oil** *(lighter olive oil will be less bitter)*
- **Salt**
- **Pepper**
- **Vegetable broth**
- **Onions and peppers** *(optional)*

Know ye mortals the mystery of the punished plantains. Boiled, fried, and mashed… this monstrous banana acts like a potato for you to feast. The mystic fruit eaten daily by those in the Caribbean shall unfold its secrets before you.

This is one of the unholy trinity of plantains: Tostones – Double fried green plantains. Maduros – Ripe fried sweet plantains. And Mofongo – boiled, fried, and mashed green plantains and/or yuca.

Let us gaze upon the oracle to begin.

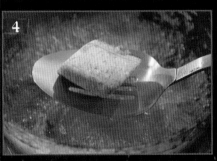

Mofongo of Disharmony

1. Rend the outer flesh from the green plantains. Cut them into thumb-sized pieces and cut a slit in the thick skin from bottom to top. Cut around the inside to remove its skin and expose the inner treasure. Boil these for about ten minutes. Fear not, they will not be soft upon completion of this. All is well.

2. Whilst the plantains are scalding in the boiling water, prepare a second pot for the garlic oil sauce. Fill a bit with olive oil and grate plenty of garlic in. Turn the heat to a low temperature not to exceed the numbers one or two. The concept here is not to toast the garlic, but to invoke the gods of heat to spread the powerful flavor of garlic throughout. Use a lighter olive oil for less wrath of the bitter taste gods.

3. Remove the plantains from their boiling bath and fry them a bucket of scalding oil! The torture will not end.

4. While the plantains fry to a light golden brown, optionally sauté a bit of onions and peppers. Season with salt and pepper. Dump them in the oil garlic sauce pot after done.

5. Dump your fried plantain pieces into your original pot. Mash them with your mace until crushed by the gods. Add your oil garlic sauce and vegetable broth to moisten this concoction. This dish wins no awards for best looking but one taste and you shall succumb to the addiction.

101

YUCA

SPELL REAGENTS (INGREDIENTS)

- **Yuca**
- **Olive oil** *(go lighter for less bitter)*
- **Fresh garlic**
- **Onions**
- **Salt**
- **Pepper**

Yuca is so fucking metal, it makes its own cyanide! I am not kidding. Luckily, the type of yuca purchased to eat do not have as much cyanide. This metal as fuck root makes you even more metal by eating it and defying death.

Be not deceived by the simple elegance of this dish. How can such basic things pack so much flavor? The secret lies in the method of this ritual.

This is glorious as the main feeding ritual or a sacred side:

Call of the Yuca Moon

1. This is yuca. It stands before you bold, defiant, waxy, shiny, hard, and seemingly inedible. To strike a blow into the heart of this root, a large sturdy knife is preferred. I like a trusty battle axe, but you must find your own weapon of choice. Cut the outer brown layer off the ancient root. It reveals a clean white underbelly. If this is very brown, or smells incredibly strong, it shall be quite bitter. I suggest you cast it aside, for age may have taken it. Skin them, and cut them into a suitable size for one's mouth.

2. Boil the yuca in a pot of lightly salted water. When your time-piece claims 25-30 minutes have passed, they should be fairly soft, and flaking apart when stabbed. Taste it; it should already be delicious.

3. Whilst the yuca boils, you shall prepare the ultimate garlic sauce. Heed these words, mortals! Turn the heat of your burner to a mere sham of Satan's fire (low or one). Pour forth a good amount of olive oil. Virgins are always a good sacrifice, et alone extra virgins. Yet before you reach for the extra virgin olive oil, know that it has a chance of running bitter. Go with a regular or lighter olive oil for less bitterness and sorrow. If you are used to the robust taste the extra virgins offer, indulge fully. Grate in an entire bulb of garlic, and cut some rings of onions. It shall heat lightly and and the flavor shall flow throughout.

4. Drain the yuca from its bubbling hot spring, and mix the garlic sauce and the cyanide root together. Cover well with salt and pepper to taste.

FIDEO

SPELL REAGENTS (INGREDIENTS)

- **Fideo** *(either coil or short)*
- **Fresh tomatoes**
- **Tomato sauce**
- **Vegetable broth**
- **Chipotle peppers** *(canned in adobo sauce)*
- **Salt, pepper, and cumin**
- **Olive oil**

Walk down the sacred halls of a Latin food market or the Hispanic aisle of your grocery store and your eyes probably will not even see what is in front of you. Perhaps in passing you may have noticed there was a pasta there, but never thought anything of it. Most do not equate pasta with Mexican or other Latin American food within their dark mind, yet it is a common dish.

The chipotle peppers in adobo sauce carry the flavor of this dish. Do not go so heavy on the other spices for they are of minor importance.

Years of Silent Fideo

◀ 1. This is fideo. You will find it in the Hispanic aisle of a grocery store. It is cheap as all fuck.

Heat some olive oil in a pan to a medium low heat and begin to toast the fideo until it turns a medium brown. Do not let the spirits of the stove char it. A bit blackened like the depths of the abyss is okay, but not blackened like your soul.

2. Invoke some fresh tomato pieces. I use a medium-sized tomato for a package of fideo.

After sautéing the tomatoes around for a bit, add your pasta sauce and two sliced-up chipotle chilies from the can. The remainder of the chilies mummifies their freshness in the refrigerator for quite some time in a plastic sarcophagus.

Two to three chilies provides the flavor of the ages. More than this shall push you into chipotle crimson hell.

Call upon the vegetable broth and a bit of cumin to cover it all in a liquid deluge. Bring this to a boil.

Cover, reduce your heat to low, and simmer like the hot springs of the gods.

3. When dried, and the noodles are soft, the fiery meal awaits your calling. Add some salt and pepper if needed…then feast!

*The company in this picture does not endorse this book or the Vegan Black Metal Chef project.

CHIPOTLE FAJITAS

SPELL REAGENTS (INGREDIENTS)

- **Various fajita vegetables**
  (bell pepper, onion, carrots, mushrooms, zucchini, etc. – pick a few)
- **Seitan or other vegan meat** *(optional)*
- **Chipotle peppers** *(canned in adobo sauce)*
- **Corn or flour tortillas**
- **Cooking oil** *(I use olive oil or a neutral oil like canola oil for this... but it does not matter very much)*

SPICES

- **Garlic or garlic powder**
- **Salt**
- **Pepper**
- **Onion powder**
- **Cumin**
- **Chili powder or fresh chilies**

- **Smoked paprika** *(optional)*
- **Fajita seasoning blend** *(optional)*
- **Any seasoning blend you want...**

Other items to eat with your fajitas, see above

Fajitas to War

The vegetable fajita rite is merely the tip of a full fajita seance. The other incantations—making beans, guacamole, rice, fresh salsa or pico de gallo—all combine together for the ultimate unholy meal. The beans and rice take almost no work after putting them up to cook. This and the guacamole are the only items that require attention. As with any manifestation that combines many things, the salt and spices combine over dishes. This means don't fucking use as much as you would on its own.

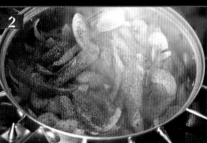

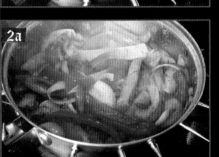

1. Butcher your vegetables into stalks like a creature possessed. If using zucchini, hold it back from the flames for a few minutes after committing the other vegetables. You do not want to cook zucchini for very long. If using seitan or another vegan meat like tofu, brown them first in the fires and fat.

   Sauté the vegetables in your cooking oil. You are not going to sauté the fuck out of them. You want them slightly fresh and crisp as if rigor mortis had just set in. They shall not be wilted and pathetic.

2. Spice the vegetables with reckless abandon. Use whatever spices sound good to you in fajitas. Do not fear spice blends. These are often cheap and awesome.

3. Optionally, add sliced chipotle peppers from your can. Beware, they overpower the taste quickly, so use temperance with these. Two or three go a long way; store the remainder of the chipotle peppers refrigerated or frozen in the depths of hell for a long time.

   The daemonic clock ticks quickly with this. Sauté until they look awesome, but then remove before the dark ones steal too much of the crisp essence.

Gather around your other implements of fajita sacrifice!

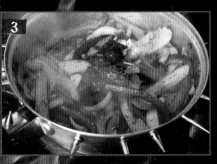

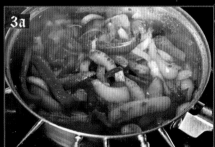

SPINACH & BEAN ENCHILADAS

SPELL REAGENTS (INGREDIENTS)

FOR ENCHILADA SAUCE
- **Olive oil**
- **Flour** *(or corn flour)*
- **Tomatoes** *(2-3 roma or 1-2 medium/large other tomato)*
- **Tomato paste**

FOR THE BEANS
- **Can of vegan refried beans**
- **Olive oil**
- **Sriracha or other hot sauce** *(optional)*

FOR THE SPINACH
- **1 bag of spinach**
- **Olive oil**
- **Onion**
- **Fresh garlic or garlic powder**

- **Vegetable broth**
- **Chili powder**
- **Spices** *(salt, pepper, cumin, Italian seasoning or other dried herbs, adobo garlic powder, any spice blend)*

- **Spices** *(cumin, Italian seasoning, garli powder, any spice blend you want... go easy on the spices here though)*

- **Salt**
- **Pepper**
- **Vegan cheese shreds** *(optional)*

Opus A Enchilada

Once again, the simplicity and dark beauty manifests in unholy perfection. While requiring several small steps, each one is simplicity itself. One warning pervades over this ritual. Beware the accumulation of salt! Since this is several spells layered together, the salt will accumulate with each incantation. Now, do not fear salt, it is needed. However, let not the heavy hand of salt make each summoning so flavorful that when combined, they are too powerful for even the strongest warrior.

Summon the beans as in the tacos video. Just get a can of beans, heat them up with olive oil, sriracha, cumin, garlic powder, and Italian seasoning. Do not flavor these so strongly. Again, each item shall be only mildly spiced so the sauce carries the flavor.

1. The enchilada sauce is the master key to this whole dish. Sauté a large spoonful of flour in some olive oil. Fix your attention upon it, for if you turn away, Satan shall claim it. It will turn brown in a mere moment. This is your sign to proceed.

2. With haste, add in your vegetable broth, some diced tomatoes, and a blood smear of tomato paste. Season this with your salt, pepper, cumin, dried herbs, and whatever other spices you have chosen. The sauce carries forth much of the flavor of this dish, so do not be afraid to make it awesome.

3. The sauce shall cook down to a semi-thick pile of coagulated gore. CONTINUED

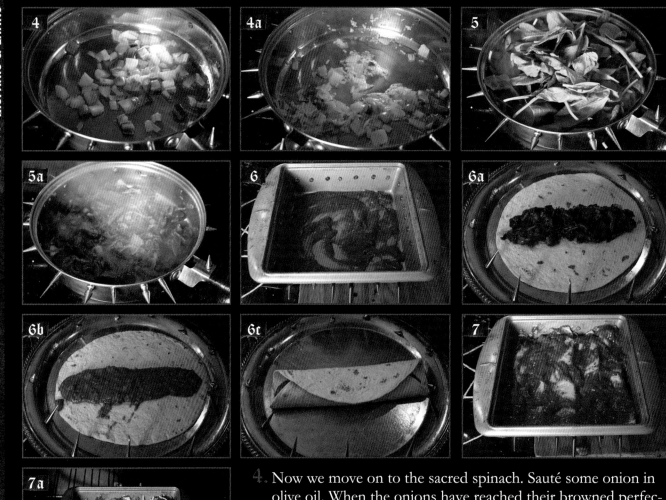

4. Now we move on to the sacred spinach. Sauté some onion in olive oil. When the onions have reached their browned perfection, grate in some garlic immediately before adding the spinach. Heed this warning, mortal…the garlic shall burn and your life will be bitter hell if you do not add the spinach with haste.

5. Add the spinach, and quickly start stirring around to mix everything up. The spinach wilts like a desiccated corpse. Cook the spinach down to a withered heap and season lightly with salt and pepper.

6. Sauce the bottom of your sacrificial baking pan with your now ready splatter of sauce. Fill thine tortillas with spinach, bean, or whatever the hell you made. Fold in the ancient way and place for sacrifice with the seam side down upon your pan.

7. Cover thoroughly with much enchilada sauce, optionally top with vegan cheese and bake in the oven fires at 350-400° F (180-205° C) for about 10–20 minutes. Invoke the broiler in the final moments for maximum crispness.

Serve with rice and beans, or pizza, or whatever the fuck else you are having. Liberate your mind to serve with whatever the fuck you want…or nothing at all.

WHY VEGANISM IS THE BEST SINGLE ACTION

I can hardly think of another way a person can make so much of a difference in the world than going vegan. One lifestyle path, not needing the actions of anyone else, which has innumerable consequences. The following article will not cite any studies, lay out any disputable statistics, or otherwise suggest anything subtle and hard to detect. When looked at from even an "armchair" perspective, the conclusions are obvious.

First of all, let's think about the cost of health care. Now, it's well known that one can be a junk food vegan and that all vegan food is not necessarily a "health food." There are vegan cakes, pies, "n-ice cream," fried food, sugar, preservatives, snack crackers and cookies.

Having said this, however, ask yourself this question. Would the cost of health care be far less expensive or far more expensive if everyone in your country were vegan? The answer is still obvious. The cost of health care would plummet.

If everyone switched to a plant-based vegan diet and brought consciousness to their actions, it is my opinion that incidences of heart disease, obesity, type-2 diabetes, along with many other preventable illnesses would be drastically reduced.

Something strange might arise: health care might become so inexpensive that there might be an abundance of resources to treat all those with genetic and less preventable illnesses of all types.

The debate over universal health care in the United States and other countries is a heated one where people try to distribute extremely limited resources and expensive treatments. The cost of funding this is already astronomical and growing. Even if we only lessened the incidence of heart disease and obesity, just imagine the cost savings.

One does not even have to be a "health nut" while on a vegan diet to overall eat much better and be far more healthy than the standard American diet.

Second of all, veganism helps solve the issue of world hunger and the increasing cost of food.

People in western countries only enjoy the amount of meat they currently eat at the current price because of intensive factory farming of animals, and the use of agricultural land to feed these animals that could be feeding many times more people.

Just think about how much more a cow or even a chicken has to eat to make a relatively small amount of food for people. These cows are not being fed grass and grazing upon the open hills, nor are the chickens eating various seeds and insects from the ground. They are both being fed corn and soybeans (among other grains and even ground up pieces of cow and chicken). These plants could be used much more efficiently to feed people instead.

If the same amount of farmland was used, this would create a large surplus of some plant based foods, decreasing the prices around the world dramatically. Again, no studies or statistics are needed because it's so obvious.

If everyone in India and China adopted the same diet as Americans (as they increasingly are), the current American food model would quickly become unsustainable.

What if this simple action of veganism not only decreased the food prices for everyone in the world, but helped cure one of the most disgusting problems of all? The sad truth is that currently people in the world do not starve because there isn't enough food. They starve because they cannot afford the food that is available and all around them.

Lastly, bring your attention to the cutting back of pollution and use of energy and water sources in general.

Whether you care or believe in human-caused global warming or not is irrelevant. Everyone on the other hand wants to breathe clean air, drink clean water, and have energy be affordable.

The obvious fact is, there is tremendous waste in the consumption of animal products as opposed to a vegan diet. All of the fuel, water, and human labor used to manufacture and transport the feed to the animals as well as the fuel, water, and human labor to manufacture and transport the animals to make into food for humans would be conserved.

Lakes of animal manure and factory farm waste will be no more (a huge contributor of methane gas and other greenhouse gases).

Animals must eat many times their weight in food to produce the same amount of food for humans. This means that all of the inefficiencies and use of resources that go into this process is horridly wasted in relation to its plant-based alternative.

Just think for a moment of all the meat consumed in the world. All the fast food restaurants, all of the slow food restaurants, all of the grocery stores, everything of that nature. Each bit of meat, dairy, and all animal products represent a mountain of wasted resources. Who knows, with such inefficiency eliminated…there might just be abundance for all.

This is of course just the tip of the iceberg. It does not even touch on such obvious topics as the hormones pumped into meat, resistant germs from antibiotics, and non-objective topics such as ethics, etc.

There are many other grave problems in the world such as human trafficking, racism, and other things of that nature that need to be solved. However, many of these problems cannot be solved without policing, changing of other peoples actions and many things beyond one's immediate control.

In contrast, the three main problems mentioned in this article are really an easy fix in which you are directly part of the cause or directly part of the solution…

What could you possibly have more control over than what you put in your mouth?

> **Veganism can solve or help significantly solve several of today's most pressing problems.**
> - Cost of health care
> - World hunger
> - Greatly aid in cutting back pollution

Oracle of Inspiration

Cilantro Lime Rice

SPELL REAGENTS (INGREDIENTS)

- Medium grain rice
- Lime
- Cilantro
- Salt
- Olive oil
- Vegetable broth or water

Make your rice in the usual way. Boil two cups of vegetable broth or water for one cup of rice, add a bit of salt, some olive oil, and squeeze in the juice of one lime. Add in the rice when boiling. Cover, reduce your heat to low, and simmer for 15–20 minutes. Remove from the heat and let sit for three to five minutes.

Chop up some cilantro into little bits. Add to the rice after it's done.

Tomato Fideo Soup

SPELL REAGENTS (INGREDIENTS)

- Fideo or angel hair pasta
- Olive oil
- Chipotle peppers (canned in adobo sauce)
- Pasta sauce
- Vegetable broth
- Salt
- Pepper
- Garlic or garlic powder
- Cumin
- Fresh cilantro (optional)
- Chickun-style seitan (or other vegan meat) (optional)
- Any vegetables you would like in a soup (optional)

Follow the same concepts and methods for the fideo in this section (toasting the fideo etc., on page 104). When you add the vegetable broth, add enough to make a soup. Mix with some water so it is not too salty. You can go with an additional chipotle chili here as the soup thins out the flavor.

Boil until the noodles are soft.

Scan for updates.

Oracle of Inspiration

Tostada

SPELL REAGENTS (INGREDIENTS)

- Tostada shells
- Refried beans
- Vegan meat *(optional)*
- Lettuce
- Tomato
- Avocado
- Vegan salad dressing *(optional)*

- Hot sauce or sriracha *(optional)*
- Anything you would put on a taco
- Spices for your beans *(cumin, garlic powder, pepper, herb blend or Italian seasoning, anything else)*

Prepare the refried beans using the methods in this section (page 94). Follow the same concepts for the tacos or fajitas. It's the same fucking thing eaten in a different way. These are tostada shells. They are cheap as fuck, and you get a ton of them.

Pile everything on top, put some salad dressing on that shit and eat.

*The company in this picture does not endorse this book or the Vegan Black Metal Chef project.

Quesadilla

SPELL REAGENTS (INGREDIENTS)

- Tortillas
- Vegan cheese *(either commercial vegan cheese or nut cheese)*
- Vegan meats *(optional)*

- Vegetables *(onions, bell peppers, etc.)*
- Spices *(salt, pepper, garlic powder, cumin)*
- Olive oil

This is basically a Latino grilled cheese sandwich. Use the concept of processing vegan cheese or make your own nut cheese. Both are in the Euro-American section (page 40 or 42). Sauté the vegan meats first over a medium heat. If using seitan, make sure to brown the fuck out of it. Then sauté the vegetables when the meats are almost done. Put between two tortillas with the vegan cheese. Heat up a small amount of olive oil in a pan. Put the tortilla sandwich in the olive oil until the bottom tortilla is crisp. To flip the quesadilla, hold a plate over the quessadilla in the pan. Use your spatula to go under the quesadilla and rise it up pressing it to the plate. You can then flip the plate around and scrape it off with your spatula to sauté the other side. Consume with a vengance.

113

Introduction – Indian

Indian food is so damn tasty it makes you want to run naked through the streets, and bow down to worship Krishna. This culture knows what the hell it's doing with food.

Indian food is naturally a bastardized term. The foods in this chapter hail from India, Pakistan, Afghanistan, parts of the Middle East, and various cultures that share their blasphemous spot upon the globe. For the sake of simplicity, and to piss people off…it shall be called Indian food.

Indians have made a spice powder or seed mix out of damn near everything on earth. There's a cantaloupe powder, pomegranate seed powder, mango powder, mustard seed, etc…among others. There are so many damn powders, I would not be surprised to see pickled blueberry powder "picked from a sacred Indian riverbank during holy festivals" in an Indian market.

Many cookbooks or recipe sites will have you believe that the only spices in Indian food are coriander, turmeric, cumin, and maybe fennel. While these ingredients are often present, there are just a few more…

- Aniseed
- Mace
- Green Cardamom
- Almond
- Coconut Powder

- Fenugreek Seed
- Cinnamon
- Nutmeg
- Black Pepper
- Mustard Seed

- Fenugreek Leaves
- Carom
- Clove
- Amchur Powder
- Nigella Sativa

- Pomegranate Seed Powder
- Allspice
- Asafoetida or Hing
- And Many More…

To conquer this realm, we are going to cheat and it shall be glorious.

The companies in this picture do not endorse this book or the Vegan Black Metal Chef project.

We shall venture into the land of the Indian store and purchase premade curry powders, seed mixes, and pastes. Most of these are awesome in their own way, and you shall learn to control them all. With a small initial investment of twenty-dollar coins of your realm, you will have enough spices for a year's worth of Indian food. Once acquired, you can infuse its dark flavor into whatever you wish.

The most important concept of this land shall be: how to metamorphosize Indian spice mixes. Indian spice mixes and curry mixes will get you 75 percent of the way there, but will lack something as a final product. Here they shall exhibit flavors of the highest order. You will not take all these actions every time you use a spice mix, but you may very well perform several of these ritualistic purifications at once.

Salt – Indian spice mixes do not come with the requisite amount of salt. Most have too little. Because Indian food is very reliant on the right salt amount, you will need to experiment with the taste tentacle that resides in your mouth. Just the right amount of salt brings out the taste an incredible amount. Too little and it will not grant total satisfaction despite the large amounts of other spices.

Fresh Cilantro – This is another huge staple in Indian cooking. If you throw a dragon's claw of fresh cilantro leaves in toward the end, it will give your dish a divine taste and look of vanity.

Garlic or Garlic Powder and/or Ginger – Fresh garlic and garlic powder have different effects when cooking. Which is better? They are both awesome. Ginger powder…fuck that shit. Useless garbage. If your curry is tasting dull, chances are you left out garlic and/or ginger. Most people know how to peel and chop garlic, but many are intimidated by ginger; let us dispel its mystery. Buy a "branch" of ginger at the grocery store. Snap off a one-inch section or so. Using a magic blade, scrape off the outer brownish layer or skin. Chop, grate, or blend this yellowish morsel into the food while cooking.

Sugar – A dash of sugar added to a dal or sweet potato dish punches up the flavor incredibly. Fuck it, put sugar in lots of shit.

Mustard – A little bit will go a long way.

Fresh Chilies or Chili Powder – Like fresh garlic and ginger above, an added dose of fresh chopped chilies can make your Indian food transcendent. Shop around and try out a few different chili powders to find a brand you like. All chili powders are not created equal.

Add Some Vegan Butter at the End – Vegan butter, in case you're a virgin to all this meatlessness, comes in several varieties, but most often is some kind of solidified oil blend. It is amazing enough to put on plain pasta with salt. But it's also great in more complex dishes, like Aloo Palak or Chana Masala. Vegan butter gives these dishes, and others, a smooth, "oily" look and taste; add it toward the end of your cooking. If you don't have vegan butter, try a rich oil like safflower, sunflower, or even coconut oil.

ASIAN INDIAN FRIED CAULIFLOWER

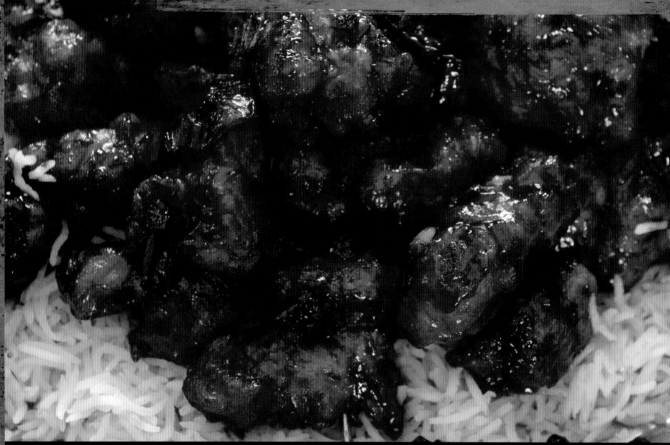

SPELL REAGENTS (INGREDIENTS)

- Cauliflower
- Ketchup
- Hoisin sauce
- Garlic
- Sugar
- Soy sauce

- Flour *(self-rising)*
- Cornstarch
- Rice flour
- Curry powder
- Green onion
- Rice *(jasmine or basmati)*

This dish looks amazing, it tastes amazing, and its sweet, crispy, savory crunch crushes souls. One sight of this perfectly-sauced deliciousness will send you into ecstatic rapture. The curry-spiced batter wins half the flavor battle while the Asian sweet sauce conquers all with its unstoppable juggernaut of taste.

There are several steps. Let us make haste upon its creation.

Grim and Frost-bitten Cauliflower

1. Boil a cauldron of water by headbanging at breakneck speed. Submerge your cauliflower to scald for 3–5 minutes. How much cauliflower? I can hear you moan... Cast runes to determine this answer. However, know that the more cauliflower head you decimate, the longer it will take to fry. Skip not this step. The blanching softens the cauliflower and allows the maximum amount of batter to stick like an eternal contract.

2. Whilst the cauliflower is boiling, start your sauce in another pot. Your pot should have spikes; it makes a difference. Start with some water and ketchup. Ketchup?!?!?! WTF, are you serious? Do not question me; just do as your overlord commands.

Add the hoisin sauce, garlic, sugar, and soy sauce. Bring this potion to a boil, reduce the heat to medium low, and keep at a slow-medium boil while the entire ritual takes place.

3. The ultimate batter for this cauliflower will be gathered. This consists of equal parts regular flour, cornstarch, and rice flour. A small amount of curry powder makes the daemons sing with delightful agony. The curry powder should compliment the taste, not overpower it. It will also make the final fried greatness shine with a golden aura. CONTINUED

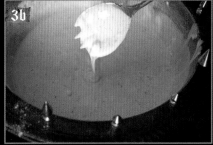

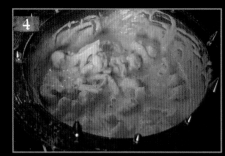

Add water to make into a semi-thick batter. Err on the thick side. This will create a batter like an exoskeleton that is semi-resistant to the sauce, and it will stay crunchy for small eons if the sauce is applied with grace.

4. Coat the boiled and drained cauliflower in the batter like a thick veil of evil. Deep fry until golden brown and as crispy as the snapped bones of your enemies.

5. At this time of your creation, your sauce should look like a coagulated, viscous pool of bubbling black blood. Watch it at times throughout this ritual, lest it burn in the fires of negligence. If yours looks like Picture 5 and has thickened well, remove from heat and set aside.

6. Heat your bits of green onion in a bare, dry, desolate pan. When slightly browned, add in the fried cauliflower and apply the sauce with perfection. It should lightly but thoroughly coat the cauliflower. To keep things crispy, apply only the perfect amount.

The final cauliflower appears before your eyes. Serve over either jasmine or basmati rice.

RICE OF THE REALM (INDIAN)

The Indian rice of the realm is unquestionably basmati rice. Use this with all Indian dishes. If you don't, you are an asshole and missing out on the synergistic perfection with the taste of curries. Go to the Indian store and ask which ones they prefer. There are many types/brands and they taste different. Either try several and settle on one, or go with their recommendation and see if you like it.

Ov the Aloo Palak and the Void

INDIAN SPINACH & POTATO

SPELL REAGENTS (INGREDIENTS)

- **Spinach** (*I usually just use one 6 or 8 oz bag*)
- **Tomato** (*one medium size or a few small roma*)
- **Red potatoes**
- **Salt**
- **Mustard seeds** (*optional*)
- **Fresh chopped garlic** (*best*) **or garlic powder**
- **Two premade Indian spice mix boxes** (*any brand any variety*) **or one mix and a standard jar of curry powder**

- **Vegan butter or a rich-tasting oil**
- **Chopped onion**
- **Chopped hot green chilies or chili powder** (*optional*)
- **Cooking oil**

CONTINUED

121

To start this off, mercilessly flay the skin from your potatoes, or if feeling lazy, just don't. Cut them into fourths or smaller and drop them into the depths of a pot of slightly salted water. Boil with the fury of your deepest hatred. Start everything else while the potatoes boil and all will be summoned forth at the correct time.

1. While your potatoes are boiling, draw your frying pan weapon and start heating some oil in your pan or wok over medium high heat. Add your devastated onion. You can also toss in a pinch of mustard seeds at this point, but using too much will summon the wrath of bitter. Invoke two of your Indian spice mixes into your pan and sauté with the onions and mustard seed (optional) for a minute or two. Recite the Bhagavad Gita backwards for maximum effect.

2. Bring forth some chopped tomato, chopped fresh garlic and green chilies (optional). Sauté everything for about two minutes.

3. The dark gods will cause the tomatoes to break down a little bit; when this happens, add a bunch of fresh spinach. Cooking spell-craft to your tastes is an art; never forget this. I typically throw a whole bag of spinach in just to make it easy. It cooks down, so if it looks like too much, just wait a minute.

4. After the spinach cooks down, the hour is right to strike. Dump your entire cauldron into a nearby blender and blend until it's a green soupy mess. Yell with a shriek from beyond as you do this. Pour the entire mess back into the pan or wok; add the boiled potatoes (but not the water you boiled them in). Now comes the last critical step…put a big-ass smack of vegan butter in there. If you are cursed not to have vegan butter, you can use a rich oil like safflower or sunflower oil or a neutral one like canola. This gives it a great smooth overall oily texture and an awesome taste.

5. Add some chili powder and salt to taste. Don't be afraid to add a touch of hellfire! Serve with paratha or naan indian bread and/or basmati rice.

Don't be a dickhead. Get basmati rice! Jasmine rice will do if that's all you have.

CHANA MASALA

The Rite of Chana Masala Invocation

SPELL REAGENTS (INGREDIENTS)

- **Chickpeas** *(either canned or soaked and boiled until soft)*
- **Tomatoes**
- **Tomato paste**
- **2 premade Indian spice boxes**
- **Fresh green chilies** *(or chili powder)*
- **Garlic**
- **Saffron** *(optional)*
- **Coconut milk**
- **Salt**
- **Sugar** *(optional)*

- **Onions**
- **Bell peppers or potatoes** *(optional)*
- **Cilantro**

CONTINUED

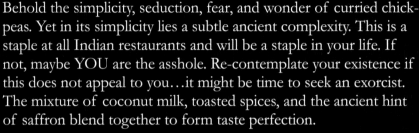

Behold the simplicity, seduction, fear, and wonder of curried chickpeas. Yet in its simplicity lies a subtle ancient complexity. This is a staple at all Indian restaurants and will be a staple in your life. If not, maybe YOU are the asshole. Re-contemplate your existence if this does not appeal to you…it might be time to seek an exorcist. The mixture of coconut milk, toasted spices, and the ancient hint of saffron blend together to form taste perfection.

Let us make haste on its summoning.

1. Many Indian (and other) recipes begin in the same way with this horrific chain of events… sauté some onions in a pan with some oil. Even the least among you can do this.

2. Invoke the wizardry of mixing two Indian spice boxes as stated in the beginning of this chapter. Sauté the spices in the oil with the onions for about a minute.

3. Now the elder gods require three of the main ingredients. Chop up some tomatoes, small green chilies (buy these at the Asian or Indian store), and fresh garlic. Toss them into your cauldron and stir as shown. Sauté for a minute or two…the time it takes to steal a lost soul.

4. The essential demonic aspect of this dish is next. Drain, rinse, and add a can of chickpeas or the chickpeas softened in a slow cooker. Sauté these for yet another few minutes.

5. Pour forth a flood of coconut milk and a dab of tomato paste. Do not use crap coconut milk! Use the canned kind. You shall quest for the can of highest calories and fat! The colors should be a creamy red orange like a blood moon. Mix this up as instructed in the Vedic texts. To impress the sages of old, add a pinch of saffron into this concoction.

6. Headbang around the kitchen in a frenzy to bring this to a boil. Cover, reduce the heat and simmer, like an unspeakable death, for at least 15-20 minutes. The longer the ritual, the more the flavors will alchemize together. A few minutes before the end of this rite, add a large handful of cilantro.

Served upon a heaping pile of corpses of basmati rice, your final creation appears.

Under the philosophy of do-able veganism, I do not advocate making most breads "from scratch." Breads often take significant time and do not leave you with multiple meals. They give you something to eat meals with.

Indian breads are damn near essential to eating Indian food, so get some Indian breads somehow. They can usually be found in either Asian or Indian stores.

In my opinion there are two main types: paratha type and naan type. Of course there are more than these, but this is a generalization.

The paratha type you heat in a pan (usually with no extra oil) on both sides until puffed out and crisped. The naan type looks more like a flat bread, toasted with vegan butter on top.

INDIAN BREAD

PARATHA

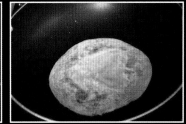

NAAN

*The company in this picture does not endorse this book or the Vegan Black Metal Chef project.

PAKORAS

SPELL REAGENTS (INGREDIENTS)

- **Chickpea flour** *(also called gram flour)*
- **Rice flour**
- **Self-rising flour**
- **Indian spice mix or two**
- Salt
- Garlic powder
- Variety of vegetables to fry
- Oil and/or deep fryer

Relinquishment of Pakoras & Flesh

1. Start, under a full moon, by putting some chickpea flour in a bowl. For every part of chickpea flour you use, add about 1/4 as much rice flour. While whispering incantations to the gods, pour in as much self-rising flour as to equal the chickpea and rice flour combined. For a blasphemous example, if you use 1 cup chickpea flour, add to it 1/4 cup rice flour, and 1¼ cup regular flour.

Now it is time to spice it up. The wicked desire flavor in their lives.

2. Add some salt, garlic powder, and one or two of your Indian spice mixes. Stir like you are churning the ashes of a corpse to blend everything in with the flour.

3. Now, summon up the waters of Hell to make it into a semi-thick batter. Eventually, it should stick to your vegetables and still be able to run off them a bit, too. It should not be holy-shit thick; add more water if it is.

Cut up the vegetables you are going to use as if to hide a victim. Use whatever the hell you want, but the ancient ones know that these are of the chosen:

- **Broccoli** • **Potatoes** • **Sweet Potatoes** • **Onions**
- **Cauliflower** • **Eggplant**

Toss your cut up vegetables in your batter like creatures drowning in tar pits…coat them well.

Turn on your deep fryer (or if you don't have one, fill a pot halfway with canola oil and heat over a medium heat. Test by dropping a drop of breading in. If it rises like the dead, it's ready). Fry until golden brown. They should come out of the fryer with a fairly thick breading on them. Serve with any curry or dunk in one of the myriad of chutneys.

MUNG BEAN DAL

SPELL REAGENTS (INGREDIENTS)

- **Mung beans** *(or any lentils)*
- **Two Indian spice packets or one and a curry powder**
- **Salt**
- **Sugar** *(optional – but highly recommended)*
- **Vegan butter or oil**
- **Cilantro**
- **Chili powder or fresh chilies** *(optional)*

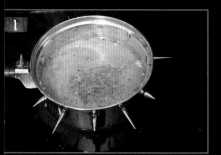

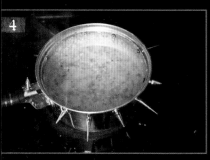

Thus Spake the Dal Spirit

The rite of dal creation is the art of crafting a delicious slop. This unholy slop becomes a meal in itself or an amazing side dish when placed over rice. It may also be used in a blasphemous manner by being scooped up with a pakora, or it makes an evil pact with Indian bread such as a paratha or naan. So inexpensive you will think yourself escaping the global food price cabal, yet filling, amazing, and easy to make. Let us begin the reading of the ancient knowledge.

1. This begins by first choosing how much lentil slop you wish to appear. Beware, for this beast increases in size by many times. I typically only make about a half-cup, which is plenty for a few meals with rice. Once the sacred amount is chosen, drown them like babies in four times as much water as lentils.

2. Once sufficiently flooded with water, add in a few shakes of the two Indian spice packs. Add a bit of sugar if you so choose. Try the sugar at least once; Satan will reward you for your decadence.

3. Bring this to a boil, cover, reduce heat and simmer like the sulfurous springs of Satan's bath. A spiked pot *does* make it taste better. If your enemies charge through the door, you can lay them to waste with this fine weapon while scalding them with lentils at the same time. No one will dare confront you with such power.

4. After about 30 minutes have passed, the time has come to add your vegan butter (or just some oil) and a handful of cilantro. Melt in the vegan butter, and stir around for a minute or two. Fully brought into this world, your final creation shall be as mesmerizing and enchanting as the pools of eternity.

ALOO MATAR

SPELL REAGENTS (INGREDIENTS)

- Red potatoes
- Peas
- Two Indian spice packs
- Fresh green chilies
- Coconut milk (*highest calorie and fat can you can find*)
- Cooking oil (*anything but olive oil*)

Born In An Aloo Matar Gown

Potatoes and fucking peas…it's just fucking potatoes and peas spiced and in coconut milk. The majestic simplicity of this recipe should not be overlooked. As always, follow the ancient concept of delicious coconut milk. It shall be the highest calorie and fat can you can find. See the Asian section on Thai curries (page 74), if you do not know what I speak of.

1. Begin by peeling and sautéing some red potatoes. Sauté them until a little bit browned.

2. Mix with perfect alchemy two premade Indian spice mixes. Sauté this in the oil until fragrant. Consummate the marriage with fresh green chilies.

3. Add the coconut milk and green peas. Stir around and bring to a boil. Cover, reduce heat and simmer as if communicating with the netherworld.

Serve with paratha and basmati rice.

TANDOORI SEITAN

SPELL REAGENTS (INGREDIENTS)

- **Vegan yogurt** *(plain)*
- **Seitan**
- **Tandoori seasoning** *(or any curry powder)*
- **Various vegetables**
- **Salt**
- **Basmati rice**

Tandoori Life Force Mysteria

This dish is the ultimate in lazy perfection. Mix the yogurt and spices, pour it over the seitan and vegetables. Bake that shit.

1. This is some vegan yogurt. Plain yogurt; not flavored. Invoke your Indian tandoori spices and some salt. Mix this shit together.

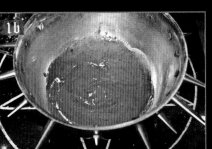

2. Cut up some seitan thinly in a pan. Smother with your yogurt and spices. Bake at 350° F (180° C).

◀ It shall appear as thus.

BECOME A ROARING FIRE

One of my favorite authors, Omram Michael Ivanov, a Bulgarian mystic, pointed out something interesting: what happens when a wind blows on a lit candle? The candle flame goes out, of course. What happens when a wind blows on a roaring flame? *It gets stronger!!!*

This concept can be applied to many aspects of our life and being. When we are weak, a little trouble comes along and is a giant disaster for us. It sets us back, and can even derail our plans. It will metaphorically "put us out." When we are strong, however, little troubles are easily conquered and make us stronger. Similar to working out at a gym, we conquer small obstacles to gain their strength. You are already a roaring fire whether you know it yet or not. Start with making a few solid decisions daily. Exercising your decision-making muscle will build upon itself. When the winds of trouble blow on you, have the conviction not to let it blow you out. Transform the energy in the trouble into fuel for your fire!

Oracle of Inspiration

Curry Roasted Potatoes

SPELL REAGENTS (INGREDIENTS)

- Potatoes
- Premade curry powders
- Olive oil

More than easy. Use the same concepts for the roasted potatoes in the Euro-American section (page 44).

For the spices, use the same methods for mixing premade spice boxes in this section.

Roast in the fires of hell for about an hour and a half at 350° F (180° C). Press the broil button in the last five minutes for crispiness.

Paratha Wrap Taco Thing

SPELL REAGENTS (INGREDIENTS)

- Anything you want on a sandwich
- Paratha

Make anything you would normally make on a sandwich or wrap. Put that shit on a paratha instead for a twist. Follow the methods for heating up a paratha in this section (page 125).

Scan for updates.

Oracle of Inspiration

Green Bean Biryani

SPELL REAGENTS (INGREDIENTS)

- Green beans
- Onions
- Potatoes
- Two Indian spice boxes
- Salt
- Chili powder *(optional)*
- Basmati rice
- Cooking oil
- Red beans *(optional)*
- Raisins and chopped nuts *(optional)*

What the hell is the difference between a biryani and any curry dish with rice? Who the hell knows? Who the hell cares? The word biryani looks good on paper and it's fun to say. Cut the ends off of some green beans and cut some onions into slivers. Skin, cut into bite-size pieces, and boil a potato or two. Use the same methods of making most of the dishes in this section. Sauté the onions and green beans together. They should not have the life cooked out of them. Sauté the spices with the onions and green beans. When the potatoes are soft, get them the fuck in there and sautéing around. Throw in an optional can of drained and rinsed red beans if the whim takes you. You can throw some beans into damn near anything like this. Don't complicate shit if it makes you hesitate; this dish is amazing without them. For a dash of sweet and crunch, optionally throw in some raisins and chopped nuts. Very optional; try it once without them. Serve over basmati rice.

Tamarind Chutney

SPELL REAGENTS (INGREDIENTS)

- Tamarind paste
- Premade Indian spice box or two
- Sugar
- A little oil
- Water

Tamarind chutney will blow your fucking mind open with flavor. This is an incredible dipping sauce, marinade, baste, and overall flavor explosion. Dip your breads or pakoras in it, or just pour it on a dish. Easy as fuck.

1. Start with heating a small amount of oil. Sauté a small amount of spices in it until fragrant. Just a few moments. The point is just to get a bit of spice in there, not to make a small curry dish.

2. Pour in some tamarind paste. It shall be thick and brown like old coagulated vomit or blood.

3. Add some sugar, and dilute the whole thing with a bit of water. It should be about one third tamarind paste, two thirds water. Bring this to a boil and simmer for five-ish minutes.

italian

Introduction – Italian

Italian food tantalizes your senses like a hallucinogenic poison that slowly rots your brain flesh. They have perfected the use of garlic in damn near everything. Garlic bread, garlic sauce, garlic in the tomatoes, garlic in the pesto, garlic fucking everywhere.

People think that all Italian food is smothered in cheese, meat and more cheese…and more meat. Those fools will be shown the error of their bastard thoughts and the path to vegan Italian decadence. From the land of high food, high fashion, and high calories, let us begin with the incantations.

I will not bore you with methods here. The main concept will be to master the sacred three sauces of marinara, pesto, and Alfredo.

All else are details.

OVEN TEMPERATURES

Anything with unlimited choices can be daunting. What fucking temperature do you cook shit at? There are many temperatures to choose from, yet I will narrow them down to the only three that matter.

350° F (180° Celcius): This will cook shit fairly slowly. This is the standard oven temperature for many things. Expect food to be in for 30-60+ minutes at this temperature. Will not boil water easily.

450° F (230° Celcius): Fairly fucking hot oven temp. This will cook things somewhat fast, but they are in danger of burning if not watched. This will boil water and seriously brown shit.

Broil: This just sets the oven coils on "balls to the wall," all-out heat. This will char shit if left unchecked, but will add an awesome crispy top layer to many things.

LASAGNA

Lasagna to the Welkin at Dusk

SPELL REAGENTS (INGREDIENTS)

- **Tahini** *(sesame butter)*
- **Lemons or lemon juice**
- **Garlic powder**
- **Salt**
- **Lasagna noodles**
- **Pasta sauce**
- **Fresh garlic**
- **Various vegetables** *(mushrooms, onions, bell peppers, anything you want in lasagna)*
- **Fried eggplant** *(optional)*
- **Vegan pepperoni** *(optional)*
- **Yellow squash** *(optional)*
- **Any other lasagna fillers you can think of** *(optional)*
- **1 or 2 types of Italian seasoning**
- **Pepper**
- **Olive oil**

CONTINUED

139

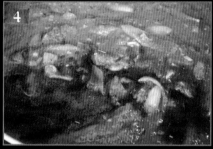

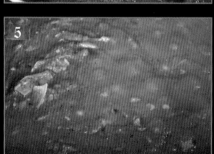

Not going to lie here: lasagna takes some time to make. Between the cooking down of the vegetables, conjuring the tahini sauce, layering of everything, and baking in the oven…plan on at least an hour before slaying and consuming this creation.

1. Cook down some onions and mushrooms in a good bit of olive oil. Use a horde of onions and mushrooms. There is nothing worse than not having enough sauce at the end of your lasagna. Cook these down on a medium/medium low heat. Since you will be making a lot of sauce and doing a few things at once, you do not want to burn your reagents with the fires of hell.

When they look like Picture 1A, it is time for the bell peppers to attack the pot.

2. Add the bell peppers to your bubbling madness. Cook them down to the depths of the abyss.

3. Now we must spice this mess while it cooks. Follow the ancient methods in the vegetable pasta recipe in this chapter to summon a mind-blowing sauce. To summarize, add a ton of fresh garlic, various dried herbs (you can just mix one or more Italian seasoning blends), salt, pepper, a touch of chili powder, optionally fresh basil, oregano and vegetable broth, as well as some fresh hot peppers if you have them.

4. Add a bloodstain of red wine to this cauldron.

◄ 5. Your sauce should look like this upon completion.

During the cooking-down process of making the sauce, you shall prepare the tahini sauce. Refer to the making of tahini sauce cooking concept in the Middle Eastern section (page 168) to learn how to do this. In short, take a few spoonfuls of raw tahini, add lemon juice (cut with water if too lemony), garlic powder, and salt. Pulse in your blender of oblivion or whisk together with a fork.

Also during this sauce preparation, boil some lasagna noodles for ten minutes in slightly salted water.

6. Prepare your lasagna pan by pouring a small amount of olive oil and mixing in a bit of sauce.

7. Begin layering your noodles, sauce and tahini. I like to spread the tahini on about every other layer. Only you will decide if you want more or less after you try it.

Keep layering! Your creation is starting to look glorious!

One of the great mysteries of this world is that somehow a box of lasagna noodles fits perfectly into a standard size baking pan. Who decided this? Did the lasagna makers fit it to the pan? Did the pan makers fit it to the lasagna? Not even the sacred tarot knows the answer to such questions.

8. Bake your final creation in your personal inferno for about 30 minutes at 350°. You can optionally make the top extra-crispy by engaging the broiler for just a few minutes. Watch the entire time while the broiler is on, lest you turn your entire meal into char! The majesty of the lasagna looks like so: ▼

CARAMELIZED ONIONS

SPELL REAGENTS (INGREDIENTS)

- **Onions**
- **Olive oil**
- **Special equipment for maximum sloth: Slow Cooker** *(see sidebar)*

Minions of the world, go to your thrift stores or second hand shops and purchase a slow cooker before this book sparks a global price explosion. Get a fucking small one. The big ones are good for making a big-ass meal, but the small ones are good for the rites of this book: caramelized onions and rising undead beans from dried beans.

Caramelized Onion Cleansing

Caramelized onions made in the traditional way are a bit of a pain in the ass. You basically chop onions into long slivers and sauté them over a low or low medium heat for about an hour. You have to constantly watch them like the guardians of the afterlife and stir them frequently, lest the hellfires claim their tribute.

This method requires no fucking work but about 12 hours of time. Start the preparation a day before.

1. Cut some onions into longish slivers. It is not a big deal how you cut them, just fucking do it. They will shrink like decaying bodies after the soul travels on to eternity.

   Pour a small flood of olive oil upon them. You cannot see the flood in the picture, but there is a small pool down there. This is also not a big fucking deal. Just get some olive oil in there.

   Cover it and set on low for about 12 hours.

2. At the moment of triumph, they shall appear as golden perfection. You cannot substitute sautéed onions for these. They have a very unique taste and add a specific quintessence to many dishes.

Add as a topping to almost any vegan meat or pasta dish.

SLOW COOKER

Find a thrift store (second-hand shop) of your realm and you shall find jewels of the kitchen for cheap as fuck. One of these jewels is a slow cooker. This is useful to have if only to do two things: 1) Make beans from dried beans. 2) Make caramelized onions. To make beans from dried, just put them in plenty of water, turn it on, and when you wake up the beans will be ready to cook in a meal or save for later. Caramelized onions are a pain in the ass on the stove, but just cut some onion into strips, put in the slow cooker and drench with olive oil. Turn it on low and overnight you shall have caramelized onions with no work.

ROASTED GARLIC

SPELL REAGENTS (INGREDIENTS)

- **Fresh garlic**
- **Olive oil**
- **Aluminum foil** *(or clay roasting pot)*

I Will Lay Down My Bones Among the Roasted Garlic

Roasted garlic can lead you to ultimate satisfaction in life. Many choose not to take the demonic pact for this victory, because they do not want to pay the cost. There is a cost for all deals with the devil. This will cost you about five minutes of actual labor, a dollar or two, and an hour to an hour and a half of total sloth.

Just like anything with a cost, it will hold the vast majority of people back even when the path is clear.

1. Prepare a sheet of foil as both an altar and a tomb. Scalp a bulb or three of garlic and pour a gushing amount of olive oil into the open wound.

2. Wrap the foil to entomb the garlic and olive oil during its journey through the fiery underworld.

3. Bake the foil garlic tomb for about 50 minutes at 400° F (205° C) or an hour and a half at 350° F (180° C).

When it emerges, it shall be soft and slightly brownish. Let it cool for a few minutes, lest you scald your black metal claw hand. Squeeze the back of them like a zit to expunge the pus into a bowl. Make sure it is all pus and no garlic husk. Stir with your demonic spork into a paste.

It is now ready for many rituals.

VEGAN WINE

What the hell is not vegan about wine? Though wine is made from grapes, it is often filtered through all sorts of crap. This can include bone marrow, fish swim bladders, egg whites, gelatin and other animal parts. Look up online whether the wine you are about to buy is vegan.

Oftentimes, a lot of the cheapest wines are vegan, and these are great for cooking and great on the budget. Whoever said, "I would only cook with a wine I would drink," was probably fucking drunk. Tons of cheap wines are great to cook with. Just make it happen; you will not be disappointed.

SUN-DRIED TOMATO PASTA

SPELL REAGENTS (INGREDIENTS)

- **Sun-dried tomatoes** *(either in the jar with oil or vacuum sealed)*
- **Roasted garlic** *(prepared beforehand)*
- **Caramelized onions** *(prepared beforehand)*
- **Pine nuts**
- **Olive oil**
- **Vegetable broth**
- **Large handful of spinach**
- **Pasta** *(I like penne with this)*
- **Salt**
- **Pepper**
- **Parsley flakes**

This is wicked easy to make and tastes amazing. However…

Beware, mortals! The watchword for this dish is preparation.

I usually do not do crazy amounts of preparation for dishes. No one likes to do it. When you want to eat, you want something, you want it now, and you might not have known what you wanted a day or an hour ago to start the preparation.

Your lazy-ass habits will be well set aside for this dish, as you can use the products of your preparation for other despicable creations.

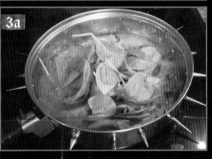

Sculpting the Throne Ov Sun-Dried Tomato Pasta

The two main things to prepare are caramelized onions and roasted garlic. If you cannot think of anything else to do with those creations, then you are a pathetic human being (who should just look throughout this book). Just like no one ever said, "I have all this extra crack to sell, and no one to buy it," no one ever said, "I have all this roasted garlic and caramelized onions and no way to eat it."

See the methods on caramelized onions (page 142) for full instruction, but as a review…basically just cut two or more onions into strips, pour some olive oil on top, and cook in a slow cooker overnight on low. This takes about 8–10 hours but is no effort at all.

Once again, see the cooking concept on roasted garlic (page 144). Cut the tops of the garlic off still in the bulb, pour some olive oil on the garlic, wrap in foil and bake at 350° F (180° C) for about an hour.

It's almost no work; make as much as you want. A little takes just as long as a lot. Once the initial rites are done, this dish could not be easier.

1. Begin by heating some olive oil in the ancient way. By the light of the moon, heat it to a medium high heat. Sauté your mushrooms and pine nuts until they are golden like the treasure of dragons.

2. Just dump in your caramelized onions, roasted garlic, and some sun-dried tomatoes. This is where all of your preparation makes this the easiest dish ever.

3. Whilst you are sautéing this perfect alchemy…heat up some vegetable broth in another pot. Add this vegetable broth and some spinach to your cauldron. Stir this all up in a fit of rage.

4. Finalize this ancient brew by spicing with salt, pepper, and parsley flakes. That is really all it needs. Everything in this dish is so damn flavorful, it will shock you into the consciousness of the one reality. Smother your pasta with a medium coat of your sauce.

Serve with a side of vengeance! Your creation manifests upon this plane of existence.

AVOCADO PESTO PASTA

SPELL REAGENTS (INGREDIENTS)

- Pine nuts
- Fresh basil leaves
- Several cloves of fresh garlic
- Salt
- Pepper

- Pasta
- Ripe avocado
- Olive oil
- Vegan chickun fingers *(optional)*

Avocado pesto pasta (like revenge) is a dish best served cold. Not cold like the frozen glaciers of solitude, but chilled like the icy peaks of the North. What initially seems like a weird combination shows its master alchemy in the end. Oily, nutty, garlicky, basily, salt and peppery pasta is as addictive as slaying hordes of your enemies. It is as delicious as feasting upon the souls of the fallen.

If you want to make regular pesto sauce, just don't put the avocado in. Let this ritual pass your lips at least once, however, lest your life remain incomplete with an avocado-shaped void in your soul.

Kings of the Avocado Pesto Pasta Creation

1. Pour a small but significant amount of olive oil in a small pot and begin to heat it upon medium high. Let not your pot of oil combust upon your stove, but get it fairly hot.

2. Once the oil is fairly hot, pour in about 1/3 as many pine nuts as you have oil. They will begin to bubble up from the depths if your oil is hot enough. Once this happens, take the pot off the heat. The residual fire within the oil will continue to toast the pine nuts.

3. Quickly, with the haste of the spirits, grate six or seven cloves of garlic into your hot oil, toasting pine nut mixture. The garlic will begin to brown and bubble. The latent heat still within the oil will toast the garlic to perfection.

4. Pour this pine nut and garlic mixture into your eviscerating blender. Add a medium large handful of fresh basil.

5. Blend this mixture like a tornado of souls.

6. Stop here if your simple mind wants plain pesto sauce. If you choose to venture into the beyond…cut open and scoop in a ripe avocado. Whir this into a smooth paste. Your green perfection will appear as in Picture 7.

7. Lightly coat some boiled pasta with your avocado pesto sauce. It should thoroughly cover it, but not be swimming in it. This much sauce will last for several large meals. You will want plenty as the addiction sets in. Add salt and pepper to match your horrid taste! Put this pasta and sauce into your refrigerator or freezer to chill. (Thou shalt not freeze it!) Optionally, top this off with your favorite heated vegan crispy chickun fingers.

Upon the hour of icy perfection, your creation should be born into the world!

FETTUCCINE ALFREDO

SPELL REAGENTS (INGREDIENTS)

- Coconut milk *(high-fat)*
- Vegan butter
- Vegan parmesan cheese
- Plenty of fresh garlic
- Vegan chicken and/or shrimp *(optional)*
- Pasta
- Salt and pepper

He Who Sought the Alfredo

Fat, fat, and fat, upon more fat, garlic, and pasta! Nothing could be more tasty. Every culture has several easy pasta dishes, and this is no exception. The cheesy, garlicky, buttery, full flavor goes great as a main dish or an infernal side. It goes without saying that you shall scald some pasta in lightly salted boiling water. Boil it until it goes limp and cries for mercy.

1. Begin by melting the vegan butter into high-fat coconut milk. If you did not see the concept on choosing coconut milk in the Thai curry section before (page 74), your goal in life is to pick the can with the highest calories and fat. Before your eyes is about half a can. Use a crap-ton of butter, about a third as much as your coconut milk. Grate in several cloves of garlic to bring about the aroma of perfection. I use about two-thirds of a bulb for half a pound of pasta. Heat this on a medium low heat and bring to a boil.

2. Acquire from the depths of your soul some vegan parmesan cheese. This is becoming widely available, so consult the oracle of the internet if needed.

3. Season with salt and pepper to taste. Go easy on the salt. The vegan butter is already a bit salty.

That is it! Drench your pasta in the alfredo sauce and call this decadence into existence.

VEGANISM IS NOT AN IDENTITY

Take nothing as an identity. You are an infinitely complex, multi-faceted individual. No collection of concepts can sum you up. If you take veganism or anything else to be your identity, you will live a stunted, constricted, incomplete life. It is tempting to take things on as an identity, to hide behind that identity as "right" and all others as "wrong." To make the world black and white, as opposed to the layers of complexity a situation may entail. You will always feel assaulted by the world if this or anything else is chosen as your identity. If they can somehow show your "identity" as wrong or inferior, or otherwise break your will…your entire world will feel threatened. Your finite, incomplete self likes that. It likes feeling assaulted. It likes an "us versus them." That is what gives the insecure part of you purpose. Any rigid identity is not staying true to yourself or reality. Observe the world, develop your principles, and put them to the test. If they fail, modify or abandon them. Either way, you will be okay. You are not your thoughts.

SHRIMP SCAMPI

SPELL REAGENTS (INGREDIENTS)

- **Vegan butter**
- **Vegan shrimp**
- **Lots of fresh garlic**
- **Garlic powder** *(optional)*
- **Salt**
- **Pepper**
- **Parsley flakes**
- **Chili powder** *(optional)*
- **Lemon or lemon juice**
- **Pasta** *(I like angel hair or linguine)*
- **Vegan white wine**
- **Green onions**

Who the fuck would have thought that there is a plant product that could emulate the texture of a sea roach? Emulating flavor is easy. The vegetable kingdom has much to choose from in terms of flavor. But a fucking Japanese yam (Konjac) slaughters all when it comes to vegan shrimp scampi. This dish is not for the calorically faint of heart. It is loaded with vegan butter, olive oil, and pasta. The same people that would cry about this probably eat cookies (baked balls of oil, sugar, and wheat). Eat the food and stop complaining. Get your ass walking around and working out so you can eat what you want. I like cookies too.

Invoking the Majestic Throne of Scampi

Begin this ritual with three pots. One to boil the pasta, one for the scampi sauce, and one to sauté the vegan shrimp. Start the water boiling for the pasta, heat the sauce pot on a medium low heat, and heat the sauté pan for the vegan shrimp sacrifice at a medium high heat. Also, chop up a ton of fresh garlic into tiny pieces. I use an entire bulb of garlic for two large meals.

1. In the sauté pan, the vegan shrimp cry out in agony while sautéing in olive oil. If you purchased frozen vegan shrimp in the lower depths of Hell for this, run some water over the sealed bag to defrost the water holding them together. While frost is metal, sticking together is not.

2. In your sauce pot, pour some white wine and add your garlic. Boil the garlic in the wine for a brief moment of eternity. Add a ton of vegan butter. Not a holy-fucking-utter-shit amount, but you *are* eating scampi. It's a butter, garlic, and olive oil sauce. Add enough butter to make a sauce for the amount of pasta you have chosen. Spice this sauce with salt, pepper, and a knife-tip of chili powder. To truly evoke the gods of garlic, add some additional garlic powder. Squeeze some lemon juice into this as everything boils together. I used half a lemon, and the other half of the lemon was squeezed over the whole thing at the end.

3. As the vegan shrimp are getting browned like the curse of the evil ones, begin to break them up. I think they are too intense to eat as a giant fucking whole shrimp-looking thing. Toss in your green onion and sauté until perfection.

4. The final moment has struck! Pour your drained pasta upon the sautéing vegan shrimp and green onion. Pour your scampi sauce on this and mix all together. To make the green specks that magically appear in vegan shrimp scampi, add copious amounts of parsley flakes.

Your final meal arrives from the netherworld! The garlic gods are truly pleased with a side of garlic bread.

VEGETABLE PASTA

SPELL REAGENTS (INGREDIENTS)

- Olive oil
- Pasta
- Various vegetables *(in this I'm using mushrooms, onions, bell pepper, green onion, and broccoli)*
- Vegetable broth *(solid preferably, but liquid will do)*
- Fresh chilies or chili powder
- Salt
- Pepper
- Garlic *(preferably fresh, but powder will do, grated or chopped)*
- Various dry herbs or Italian seasoning
- Vegan red wine
- Basic pasta sauce

This is one of those staples that is deceptively simple. We all know how to make pasta and fucking sauce, right? I do not need a diabolic oracle to know that this answer is "no." There are numerous concepts and subtleties in this most common of dishes. Never forget the ultimate concept: more vegetables does not mean more flavor. Pick three to five and be done with it. Of course you can use various vegan meats, yet this dish is incredible without them. As in all cases, sometimes great but never necessary.

Vegetable Pasta upon the Throne of the Apocalypse

1. Begin by sautéing the onions and mushrooms in plenty of olive oil. These are important to sauté first in this dish, as they will take the most time to cook thoroughly. Season them with salt and pepper while they cook.

2. Throw the rest of your vegetables into your pit of hot oil and sauté to crisp perfection. Just before adding the sauce, grate the flesh of many cloves of garlic. Now is also the time to sacrifice your fresh chilies. You will be blown away by how much fresh chilies coerce the flavor of Hades out of this dish. Chili powder will make a close second, yet try the fresh chilies at least once. Summon them into your life at any Asian or Indian store. The spiciness matters not. The flavor it adds will blow your mind. Cast in your dried herbs or Italian seasoning.

3. Vomit forth your tomato sauce, vegetable broth and red wine. This is where the serious alchemy takes place. Mix in thoroughly, and add salt, pepper, and olive oil. Boil this mixture for a few minutes whilst all the spell reagents conjoin together.

4. Add the boiled pasta to your pan, and stir together until thickened and perfect. Serve with garlic bread, salad, and spikes.

GNOCCHI

SPELL REAGENTS (INGREDIENTS)

- Potatoes
- **Flour** *(I use self-rising flour, just because I use that in so much other shit and it works)*
- **Egg replacer**
- **Some kind of sauce** *(marinara, pesto, Alfredo)*

- **Whatever you need to make the sauce** *(look through this chapter)*
- **Whatever vegetables you want with them** *(broccoli, spinach, onion, mushrooms, etc.)*

Gnocchi on Fire

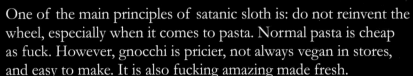

It shall be glorious!

One of the main principles of satanic sloth is: do not reinvent the wheel, especially when it comes to pasta. Normal pasta is cheap as fuck. However, gnocchi is pricier, not always vegan in stores, and easy to make. It is also fucking amazing made fresh.

1. Start with some blasphemous, heretical potatoes. I don't care what kind you use; just get some fucking potatoes. Rend their flesh to expose the innards.

2. Scald them in a boiling bath just until soft. They should be easily pierced with the mystical knife. Do not grossly over-cook, lest the waters never leave their essence. Drain them in your colander of might.

   Smash them into oblivion with your mace. Smash out all the lumps, lest they come back to haunt you.

3. Picture 3 shows egg replacer. Use whatever kind you want; just make sure it works. Many exist in this universe. Part of your life rebellion shall be to ignore the directions on the box. Just pour some in a bowl. Use your powers of divination to estimate about the amount an egg would look like after water is added. This is not a huge fucking deal. Just make it happen, and err on more rather than less. CONTINUED

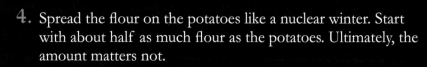

4. Spread the flour on the potatoes like a nuclear winter. Start with about half as much flour as the potatoes. Ultimately, the amount matters not.

Complete this alchemy with the egg replacer liquid mixture.

Smash and strangle everything together. Keep adding flour until the dough does not cling to your flesh.

5. Rip off a chunk of the dough and roll it into Satan's finger.

Break pieces off and roll them into Satan's balls. Don't make them too thick, for the boiling process casts an enlarging spell on these.

In another spiked bowl, lined with the ashes of the dead (or more flour), place the balls upon the ashes. Lightly coat them with the souls of the fallen.

Do this to the whole damn block of dough.

6. This is the most critical step! Boil some salted water. Drop the gnocchi in. This ritual shall not last longer than 30 seconds after they float! Alas, they are done. Toss them in your sauce.

EGGPLANT PARMESAN

Eggplant Parmesan or Vanity

- **Eggplant** *(I like the longer Chinese eggplant the best for this)*
- **Pasta**
- **Pasta sauce**
- **Vegan parmesan cheese**
- **Vegan mozzarella**
- **Self-rising flour**
- **Cornstarch**
- **Corn flour or rice flour** *(optional)*
- **Vegan white wine**
- **Vegan red wine** *(optional)*
- **Garlic powder**
- **Salt**

Fast and easy to make, indulge in this pleasure. Tradition for tradition's sake means nothing. Let us slay traditions with the ecstasy of moving into do-able veganism excellence. Fast and easy eggplant parmesan over pasta tastes like glorious fried shit mixed with a marinara-inspired mac and cheese. CONTINUED

Two strange ingredients grace these pages. Vegan parmesan cheese and vegan mozzarella. Since we are in the future, both are available. Check the multiverse of the interwebs if you cannot find them in the specialty store of your realm. **Now that you are done crying over tradition…let us begin.**

1. Before you stands the ancient ingredients of the batter. Take your choice of a thrice-great batter using self-rising flour, corn flour (or rice flour), and cornstarch…or just go with self-rising flour to keep it basic. Bring forth some salt, a mere knife-tip of garlic powder, and a bit of white wine. Flood with water until a semi-thick batter is manifested.

2. Coat the eggplant well and cast into the deep fryer for eternal torment. It has received enough punishment when it is golden brown.

3. Heat the pasta sauce to a bubbling brew. Add in the vegan parmesan cheese, optional red wine and the vegan mozzarella shreds. Melt this all into a cheesy, tomato-y glob. When fully melted, it is ready to accept the ultimate sacrifice. Bring forth the pasta!

4. Add in some of your fried eggplant and stir. Be frugal! Add only as many eggplant pieces as you are going to eat to keep the rest crisp. They should stay crisp for a short while if you only use a few at a time in the sauce.

CHICKUN MARSALA

I Am the Chickun Marsala Wizards

SPELL REAGENTS (INGREDIENTS)

- **Seitan-style chickun** *(or any appropriate vegan meat)*
- **Mushrooms**
- **Vegan white wine** *(or vegan red if that is all you have)*
- **Roasted garlic gravy** *(or flour, vegetable broth, and roasted garlic – the roasted garlic is optional but highly recommended*
- **Salt**
- **Pepper**
- **Garlic or garlic powder**
- **Italian seasoning** *(or any herb blend you choose)*
- **Olive Oil**
- **Caramelized onions** *(optional)*

CONTINUED

Anything "marsala" is essentially vegan meat with gravy wine sauce. You can take damn near any vegan meat, cover it with gravy and/or "gravy + wine" and it shall be amazing.

This is known as the sacred law of gravy.

1. Cut some seitan-style chickun into thin pieces. The thinner you cut any of the vegan meat here, the better. Not stupid thin, but when it browns like your feet upon the soil of hell the texture shall be glorious.

   Conjure the flames below your pan of olive oil and heat to a medium high heat. Cast in your thin strips of vegan meat and sauté until well browned.

2. When the hour of browning has happened, invoke the onions and mushrooms. Sauté them until both are intertwined in the matrix of cooked existence. If the evil spirits have awakened within you, optionally add some caramelized onions to this gathering.

At this juncture, there are two paths before you.

Either have some roasted garlic gravy at the ready and pour it in now, or push aside your reagents and sauté a small amount of flour in the pan until brown. If the second path is chosen, once the flour is browned, summon your vegetable broth and roasted garlic. Spice recklessly with your spices.

Pour a large deluge of vegan white wine into the pan. It will look like too much liquid at first, yet will thicken as it boils down.

It shall thicken with haste!

Serve over pasta or rice. This dish can also stand alone on its own glory with no help needed from any land.

DON'T MAKE A PROBLEM FOR EVERY SOLUTION

Some people can never get what they want in life. They won't let themselves have it, even if the path is clear. Everything that can make a situation better won't work for some reason or another.

Do not be so attached to your misery. This comes up a lot in veganism, because no matter what the array of amazing-ass food options are, no matter if you are speaking to a living, normally healthy vegan, there is always some kind of ridiculous problem that comes up in their mind.

If you don't want to do anything in life, just own the fact that you do not want to do it, or don't want to change the situation. Just own it, and bring consciousness to that. Having a problem for every solution is a way to stay in an unconscious mindset. At least owning it allows you to think about that, and face those thoughts head on with no distraction or absurd justification.

Oracle of Inspiration

Garlic Bread

SPELL REAGENTS (INGREDIENTS)

- Bread
- Vegan butter
- Garlic powder
- Herb blend
- Salt

Melt some vegan butter in a spiked plate. Dip your slices of bread in the vegan butter to saturate one side fairly well. Sprinkle with garlic powder (or optionally spread on roasted garlic). Finish with just a dash of herb seasoning blend or just some basil and oregano. Add a hint of salt.

Toast in the toaster oven. Serve with everything.

Pasta Salad

SPELL REAGENTS (INGREDIENTS)

- Pasta
- Some vegetables *(I like bell pepper and onion amongst others)*
- Italian seasoning
- Italian salad dressing
- Salt and pepper

Boil the pasta until soft. Let cool a minute.

Chop up some bell pepper and onion. Toss them in your pasta along with salt, pepper, Italian seasoning, and plenty of Italian salad dressing.

Let cool in the refrigerator.

Scan for updates.

Oracle of Inspiration

Fast Vegan Pizzas

SPELL REAGENTS (INGREDIENTS)

- **Some type of firm bread** *(French bread, bagels, flatbread, pita bread, or store-bought pizza dough)*
- **Pasta sauce**
- **Salt and pepper**
- **Garlic powder**
- **Italian seasonings**
- **Fresh basil** *(optional)*
- **Chili Powder** *(optional)*
- **Vegan cheese** *(optional)*
- **Toppings** *(whatever vegetables or vegan meats you want on your pizza)*

Since these cook fairly quickly, you will want to sauté any vegan meats beforehand.

You can make a fast pizza out of damn near anything. When I want pizza, I want it now. No waiting around for yeast to make dough rise, etc…NOW!

Fast pizzas hit the spot, even if they are not quite as fast as I want them to be. They still take about 15-20 minutes. Take some French bread (or whatever you are using as the bread for the pizza), put a spoonful of olive oil across the top and spread it around. Toss on your sauce, your toppings, your seasonings, and optional vegan cheese. If using vegan cheese, putting a small amount of vegan butter on the cheese helps it to melt better. Put this shit in the toaster oven or the oven for 10-15 minutes at 450° F (230° C) or 15-20 minutes at 350° F (180° C).

Bruschetta

SPELL REAGENTS (INGREDIENTS)

- **Good bread to toast**
- **Tomato**
- **Fresh basil**
- **Fresh garlic**
- **Salt and pepper**
- **Avocado** *(optional)*
- **Balsamic vinegar and olive oil and/or red wine vinegar & olive oil**
- **Spring salad mix** *(optional)*

If you buy a loaf of Italian bread to use for sandwiches, you will end up with several small useless pieces at either end of the loaf. These are not satisfying enough to turn into garlic bread. They are perfect for bruschetta. Toast these or any pieces of good bread. While they are toasting, chop some tomatoes into small chunks, cut up a good bit of fresh basil, and toss with them. I grate a single clove of garlic in for a fairly big batch involving three or so tomatoes. Do not underestimate the power of a single large clove of garlic. Optionally, cut up a ripe avocado into chunks. Because avocado. Apply a liberal amount of salt and pepper.

Here is where choices have to be made. I am weird. I mix red wine vinegar and olive oil into the tomato basil garlic mixture. I then apply a slight splash/stain of balsamic vinegar to the toasted bread. This does not really significantly wet the bread…it's seriously just a bit of a splash across each of them. You can just use one vinegar or the other if you want. Scoop the tomato, basil, garlic, avocado mixture on to the bread. Indulge in the freshness before you.

MIDDLE EASTERN

Introduction – Middle Eastern

Let us now turn to the ancient lands of the Middle East. The worldwide hotspot of endless strife, violence, and…um…religion (go figure) produces some incredible vegan staples. Falafel and hummus sandwiches are obviously divinely inspired. You can make these sandwiches the size of a conquered skull with all sorts of toppings, cucumber salad, hot sauce, tahini, fried potatoes, eggplant and more.

If you are not yet addicted to tahini sauce…you will be…you will be…

You can smother damn near anything in tahini sauce. Put it in a pita and it is a fitting sacrifice for your immortal self.

TAHINI SAUCE

SPELL REAGENTS
(INGREDIENTS)

- Tahini
- Lemon juice
- Garlic or garlic powder
- Salt

Wanderer Above the Sea of Tahini Sauce

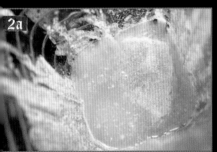

If you ripped the head and spine out of this chapter, you would find that tahini is the backbone. Tahini is not tahini sauce! You must take tahini (sesame butter) and process it into tahini sauce. If your tahini is soft, you can just use a mere hell-fork and muscle to conjure this. A blender of oblivion shall aid you if the tahini is ancient and hard.

1. Call upon some tahini. This is two or three evil spoonfuls.

2. Squeeze the juice through a strainer or colander of might to catch the larval lemon trees. They contain the bitterness of lost souls.

   Add a clove or two of garlic or some garlic powder. Bring forth some salt and prepare to claim victory.

3. Blend with the vortex of the universe with your machine or use raw muscle to prove yourself.

A dipping sauce on its own, or critical reagent for other spells.

DON'T STOP

Napoleon Hill, the great-grandfather of modern personal development, had a story. In his incredible book *Think And Grow Rich*, there is a story of a gold miner who had some initial success, but then was met with temporary defeat. He decided to quit and sell the mining equipment to a junkyard. Long story short, the miner quit three feet from finding more gold. Now I am not a firm believer that you should continue doing everything in life perpetually through constant failure, so how can we decide what to pursue further and what to give up? At any given time in life, I structure my actions on doing what excites me on an ultimate level. This will be different for everyone. No matter what you do in life, you will encounter obstacles, some degree of success, and some degree of failure. I have found, for myself, that only something that truly excites me can get me to keep going past temporary failure. If your direction is what you would be doing weather you were paid or not, don't stop, there is only ultimate success.

HUMMUS

SPELL REAGENTS
(INGREDIENTS)

- **Chickpeas** (*canned or cooked from dry*)
- **Tahini**
- **Lemons or lemon juice**
- **Salt**
- **Garlic or garlic powder**
- **Olive oil** (*optional*)
- **Different shit to put in hummus** (*optional*)

The Hummus of Mayhem

Hummus is another spell that, while easy to cast, is fucked up constantly. It is so discouraging to fail at this, that you fall into the deepest pits of despair. This sacred rite shall ensure the spell does not misfire once again.

Time to burst your mental bubble. Though it will raise the fires of anger in some, chickpeas made from dried and chickpeas from a can taste very similar.

1. Begin with a can or equivalent of chickpeas. Beware, mortal!!! **Here is a critical step!!!**

   When draining the liquid out of your can of chickpeas, capture the can liquid into a retaining vessel. If using chickpeas prepared in a pot or slow cooker, retain the water from it.

2. Here we shall use the ancient law of two's. Throw in two cloves of garlic, two large spoonfuls of tahini (not tahini sauce), and the juice of two lemons. Cast upon it a touch of salt.

3. The can water retained is now called into action. Fill the blender of oblivion with the mystic waters up to just below the top of the chickpeas. You can always add more. Too much will leave them in the realm of total mush.

4. Blend until it cries out for mercy.

   Put into your refrigerator of cooling and chill to the depths.

COUSCOUS

SPELL REAGENTS (INGREDIENTS)

- **Couscous** *(plain)*
- **Vegetable broth**
- **Olive oil**
- **Salt**
- **Pepper**
- **Parsley flakes or other herb blend** *(optional)*
- **Garlic or garlic powder** *(optional)*
- **Some vegetables to sauté**
  (if just making a simple couscous and vegetables)

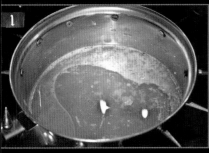

Beyond the Couscous Horizon

Sometimes the hordes are about to go to war at any moment, yet you are hungry. Couscous is one of the fastest summonings in this entire book! It works in rituals similar to rice as a bedding for other things. You will find many types of flavored couscous in most grocery stores. **Fuck these.** You can make them far better starting from plain.

1. Bring to a raging boil some vegetable broth and a quick pour of olive oil. Chant the invocations of the ancient ones with eyes rolled back into your head.

   Invoke a bit less couscous than the amount of vegetable broth.

   Stir, cover, and remove from the heat. Let this sit in solitude and despair for five minutes.

2. Sauté some vegetables in olive oil over a ghastly medium heat.

   Spice them with salt, pepper, garlic powder, and your herb blend, or whatever the fuck you want to spice your vegetables with.

3. Plain couscous is bland as fuck. The vegetable broth hath given it much flavor, however. Spice it a bit with your spices.

   Fluff with a demonic fork like a professional fluffer.

   Combine as one, with the skill of the great ones, your sautéed vegetables and couscous.

Its divine presence appears before thee.

SPELL REAGENTS (INGREDIENTS)

FROM MIX:
- Falafel mix
- Matzo meal (or panko)
- Cumin
- Salt
- Pepper
- Onion powder
- Parsley flakes

FROM FRESH:
- Chickpeas *(can or boiled from dried)*
- Fresh parsley
- Fresh cilantro
- Cumin
- Garlic or garlic powder
- Salt
- Pepper
- Any other appropriate spices you want
- Matzo meal or panko

Foreverdark Falafel

RITUAL FROM MIX:

Falafel mixes are usually only blessed by the gods of mediocrity. They are too dense and often terrible. Matzo meal lessens this horrid density. We shall combine the magic of falafel mix with matzo meal to make a worthy sacrifice.

1. This is Falafel Mix and Matzo Meal.

   Pour them into a bowl. There should be 75% falafel mix, 25% matzo mix.

   Matzo meal is bland as fuck. Use your spices to transmute this situation. Just use your master judgment and mix some of each spice in.

2. Pour in water like the breaking of flood dams. Let this sit in your refrigerator for about 15 minutes while it hardens into a texture like thick coagulated blood, suitable for rolling into balls.

   Deep fry to perfection. CONTINUED

*The companies in this picture do not endorse this book or the Vegan Black Metal Chef project.

RITUAL FROM FRESH:

Prepare your blender of oblivion upon sturdy ground.

1. Conjure a handful of fresh parsley.

   Entice a handful of cilantro.

   Captivate a small onion, chopped into fourths.

   Spice with your cumin, salt, pepper, and garlic or garlic powder. Go heavy on the spices, especially the cumin. Chickpeas are fucking bland. They need help from the spice pit.

2. Invoke a can of chickpeas and some of the can water. Do not overdo the water. You can add more as it goes. Use enough to make it blend.

3. Blend that shit into a sea of green vomit.

4. Pour into a bowl and add matzo meal (or panko). Keep adding the matzo meal until just before it is somewhat solid. Place in your refrigerator for 15–20 minutes. It shall harden like your will from many intense battles.

   After taken out, form into balls of the ancient ones and deep fry them in the pits of despair.

EVERY YES IS A NO, AND EVERY NO IS A YES

Choose your "yes's" and "no's" wisely in life, for every "yes" is a "no" and every "no" is a "yes."

Pick the direction you want in your life. If you are not picking it, it is still being chosen by your unconscious nature. Time and experience are what this life is made of. If you have no boundaries on your time you will fritter it away and wonder where it all went.

Every time you say "yes" to something, you are saying "no" to something else in your life. There is not time to do everything in the world, so choose what you actually want to do and what you want your life to look like. It is always easier and more comfortable to say "no" to things in life. "No" is the safe way. One never steps outside of their comfort zone by saying "no." Too many "no's" make life dull and boring. The correct "no's" will make your life focused and reduce bad stress. Saying "yes" and getting out of your comfort zone, toward your chosen direction, is the best kind of "yes." You need to constantly say "yes" to these new opportunities, even if they challenge you, if they bring you toward your main goals in life.

How do you know which are the correct "yes's" and "no's?" You must tap into your feeling nature. There are two types of feelings when saying "yes" to something uncomfortable. First, there is the feeling of fear, yet ultimate victory upon accomplishment. This is the type of "yes" we want to be saying as much as possible. This "yes" will make us grow. The second feeling is the sinking feeling of, "Oh, fuck." The feeling that we know we have done something wrong. Change the "yes" to a "no" ASAP if you get this feeling.

KEBAB

SPELL REAGENTS (INGREDIENTS)

- **Seitan or chickun-style seitan** *(or pre-fried, marinated tofu)*
- **Various vegetables** *(onion, bell pepper, broccoli, whatever you want on your kebab)*
- **Olive oil**
- **Cumin**
- **Salt**
- **Pepper**
- **Onion powder**
- **Chili powder**
- **Garlic powder**
- **Italian seasoning or other herb blend** *(or any spice blend or marinade you want)*
- **Skewers**

In My Kingdom Kebab

Everything is better on the grill of daemons. Open flames beckon the evil spirits to enter your food from beyond. However, kebab in the oven can be just as fatally tempting.

This ritual uses a simple baste that you do not even need to marinate. Just pour it on, bake in the fires of eternity, and its magic is cast into creation.

1. Start with a good bit of olive oil. Invoke your spices into the oily depths. Satan likes cumin, so go heavier on the cumin. Go lighter on the salt of the earth. Everything else shall be used with the moderation of the judges. The natural flavor of the baked vegetables will carry much of the taste and glory.

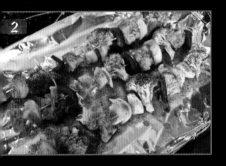

2. Skewer everything like Vlad the Impaler. Murmur incantations of evil as each pike is passed through the victims. Place on a ritualistic baking pan and dump the baste upon the impaled bodies. Bake in the oven of despair at 350° F (180° C) for about 30–40 minutes. Turn the screaming chunks at least once throughout the torture. Taste one upon the ending of this time. It shall be sinfully flavorful.

Serve upon a rice pilaf of the ancients.

LIBERATE YOUR PERCEPTION

Veganism is about liberation. Not only animal liberation, but liberation to experience a whole new set of food and lifestyle choices. If you are just now committing to veganism, take the first month or two to liberate yourself to spend extra money on ingredients to cook new things, or go to restaurants where you'll try new dishes. Remember always, you are liberating yourself to live without the baggage that comes with animal consumption and exploitation. You are liberating yourself to live consciously, and that consciousness will eventually allow you to get what you want in all aspects of your life. There is no such thing as a strict vegan diet. Strike that idea from your mind. There is nothing strict about eating a bunch of amazing plant-based food.

GYRO/SHAWARMA

SPELL REAGENTS (INGREDIENTS)

- **Seitan** *(recommended, or any vegan meats)*
- **Spring mix**
- **Tomato**
- **Cucumber**
- **Tahini or tzatziki sauce**
- **Pita bread**
- **Cumin**
- **Salt**
- **Pepper**
- **Onion powder**
- **Garlic powder**
- **Cinnamon** *(very optional)*
- **Olive oil** *(or any cooking oil)*
- **Sriracha or other hot sauce** *(optiona*

Gyro Kali

Every culture seems to have an awesome sandwich. This one has made a deal with the devil for flavor. The combination of spiced seitan, the fresh vegetables and the creamy cucumber sauce send this shit over the edge. Declare a jihad upon shitty tasting food.

There is sadly, however, one bit of preparation.

You must have already made some tahini or tzatziki sauce (look in this chapter).

Begin this infernal ritual by cutting your cucumber into small squares and soaking them in your tahini or tzatziki sauce.

1. Thinly slice some seitan. It does not have to be crazy thin; just make it happen. Sauté it in olive oil over a medium low heat. Be vigilant and guard from the devouring flames; make sure it does not burn in the charring heat of the boiling oil.

   Sauté well on both sides and spice each side with your spices.

2. Toast some pita bread and lay them upon it.

   Bring forth spring mix and tomato slices. Complete the glory with cucumber tahini or tzatziki and hot sauce.

Wrap the ass end of it in foil. This gets messy. It shall be unbelievable.

MATZO BALL SOUP

SPELL REAGENTS (INGREDIENTS)

- Matzo meal
- Egg replacer
- Salt
- Pepper
- Garlic powder
- Onion powder
- Vegetable broth
- A bit of oil *(any kind)*
- Any type of pasta *(optional)*

Hear me now!

Most people across the realm and through the ages have no idea how good this shit is. Once you have had it, matzo ball soup will constantly blow your fucking mind.

These do not expand as large as the "traditional," non-vegan version. If you have never had it, you will not care because these are fucking great. This is easy as fuck and makes many meals. I add pasta or noodles to give an excuse to consume all of the awesome broth.

Cruelty Brought thee Matzo Balls

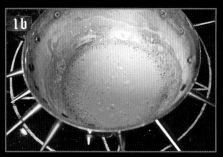

1. Follow the laws of egg replacer stated many times throughout this text. They are as follows: pour forth a bit of egg replacer powder into a bowl. Add the waters of life to be about as much liquid as an egg. Stir with reckless abandon. At this mystic hour, add a bit more water and a quick pour of oil.

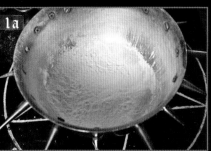

◀ 2. This is matzo meal. Call upon the matzo meal in your bowl until it is a thick, sticky mess. Season this mess with salt, pepper, garlic powder, and onion powder. Lock the concoction away in your hellish refrigerator for 10-15 minutes whilst it sets and the liquid absorbs into its soul.

Remove and form into balls. Glorious balls. Balls that glisten in the moonlight.

◀ **Balls.**

3. Bring your vegetable broth to a raging boil. Choose your pasta wisely and cast in with your matzo balls. Cover, reduce heat, and simmer in despair for about 20 minutes.

*The companies in these pictures do not endorse this book or the Vegan Black Metal Chef project.

183

BABA GANOUSH

SPELL REAGENTS (INGREDIENTS)

- **Eggplant**
- **Tahini sauce** *(tahini, lemon juice, salt, garlic)*
- **Liquid smoke**

Most baba ganoush sucks ass. If you try it at various places, it usually has a weird taste, a weird texture, and is kinda bullshit. So if you have tried baba ganoush in the past and claim to not like it, the dark ones understand.

However, this is the best fucking baba ganoush in existence. It defies all those who have come before it.

Like so many Middle Eastern dishes, you should make this before you are hungry. It takes almost no work, but it needs about an hour of time to make, and even longer to chill in the 9th circle of hell.

You also need tahini sauce. Tahini sauce is not just tahini. You will kick yourself for eternity for mistaking the two. The ritual for tahini sauce lies within this chapter of text (page 168).

Baba Ganoush of Forbidden Light

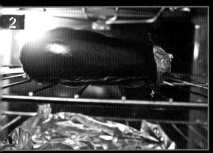

1. This spell is beyond simple. Take a fucking eggplant. Don't do a fucking thing to it.

2. Put that shit in the oven right on the tortuous rack. To catch its leaking fluids, place a piece of foil underneath it on the rack below. Fold the sides on the foil up to catch all of the bile.

   Press the broil button to invoke the hottest flames of eternity. Broil on high for an hour. Eggplant skin can withstand endless heat. When invoking the fiery daemons from beyond, they fear the eggplant for its immunity.

3. Take it out, and place it in your spiked bowl. It is often a bit limp, and some of the outside is crisp. It does not have to look limp, though; different eggplants react in deceptively different ways. Slit it open to expose its putrid flesh and scoop the innards into a bowl.

   Don't get too much of the liquid, but don't freak out if you get a bit in there. Drain the liquid like the blood of a corpse for embalming. Pieces of the skin will taste like charred death. Pick them out as you would expunge a splinter in your soul.

   Add two spoonfuls of tahini sauce, and a good bit of liquid smoke. Place in your ghastly refrigerator until its heart is chilled to the depths.

Behold the best baba ganoush you will ever have.

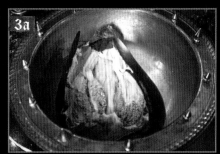

EGGPLANT, TOMATO & CHICKPEAS

SPELL REAGENTS (INGREDIENTS)

- **Eggplant**
- **Tomato**
- **Chickpeas** *(optional)*
- **Onions**
- **Fresh garlic** *(at least one bulb to make roasted garlic)*
- **Olive oil**
- **Cumin**

- **Salt**
- **Pepper**
- **Chili powder**
- **Paprika**
- **Italian seasoning** *(or a blend of dried herbs)*
- **Liquid smoke**
- **Olive oil**

The blend of flavors in this dish is uncanny. The spices take your being to uncharted depths, but the final blow to the senses is delivered by the roasted garlic and liquid smoke. This dish is cheap as all fuck, and you shall be as satisfied as the dark prince himself.

The Eggplant No Longer Rises

1. This ritual begins with cutting an eggplant into pieces and putting it into your baking crucible. Pour a torrent of olive oil upon these satanic slices. Eggplant absorbs a lot of oil, so you shall not see a pool of oil at the bottom. Spice the fuck out of it with your spices. Save the liquid smoke until the end. Either have some roasted garlic already made or prepare its fate now. See page 144 to learn this rite.

Place all in your hellish oven and bake at 450° F (230° C). Wait 10-15 minutes before beginning the next phase of the magic.

2. Heat some olive oil in a pan over the ubiquitous "medium" heat. First sauté the onions to a a translucent oblivion. Spice them with the same set of spices as the eggplant. Again, the liquid smoke shall be saved until the final moments.

Call upon the tomato into this dish and fry until they release their liquid innards. Bring forth a drained can of chickpeas and sauté for several minutes until all looks like the victory of the dark armies.

3. About this time your eggplant shall begin to look like roasted corpses. The pan is your heaven, and your oven is your hell. Combine them together for a battle of the gods. Add several splashes of liquid smoke and stir upon it. If the roasted garlic is ready, squeeze it into the concoction and stir around. If not, it shall become worthy of your sacrifice as this bakes.

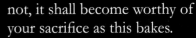

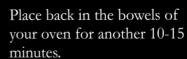

Place back in the bowels of your oven for another 10-15 minutes.

Serve with the rice pilaf of death.

Oracle of Inspiration

Tzatziki Sauce

SPELL REAGENTS (INGREDIENTS)

- Vegan yogurt
- Cucumber
- Lemon or lemon juice
- Salt
- Garlic powder

Cut the cucumber into small bits. Mix all of the ingredients with half a lemon.

Personally, I like just mixing tahini with the cucumber bits better than the vegan yogurt.

Scan for updates

Different Types of Hummus

SPELL REAGENTS (INGREDIENTS)

- Chickpeas
- Tahini
- Lemon
- Salt
- Roasted garlic
- Sun-dried tomatoes, fresh basil, and pine nuts

Be fucking creative! Experiment around with shit!

Follow the same methods as the hummus (page 170). Add in some other shit!

Oracle of Inspiration

Bagel with Hummus and Guacamole

SPELL REAGENTS (INGREDIENTS)

EVERYTHING YOU NEED FOR GUACAMOLE
- A ripe avocado
- Lime
- Cilantro
- A sliver of red onion
- A small amount of jalapeño
- A small bit of garlic
- Salt

EVERYTHING YOU NEED FOR HUMMUS
- Can of chickpeas
- Tahini
- Lemon or lemon juice
- Garlic or garlic powder
- Salt
- Bagel

Make the hummus from this section (page 170) and the guacamole from the Hispanic and Latino section (page 92).

Don't knock this shit until you try it. The combination of hummus and guac may not sound amazing at first, but there is some magic synergy with this crazy fucking blend.

Ultimate Falafel and Hummus Sandwich

SPELL REAGENTS (INGREDIENTS)

- Falafel
- Hummus
- Roasted eggplant
- Roasted potato
- Hot sauce
- Tahini sauce *(optional)*
- Cucumber and tomato *(optional)*
- Spring mix salad *(optional)*
- Baba ganoush *(optional)*

It would be too much to list all of the damn ingredients from everything.

Make the falafel from fresh or mix. Make the hummus. In the picture is roasted garlic hummus.

Make the roasted potatoes as in the Euro-American section (page 44). Roast the eggplant using the same methods as the eggplant, tomato, and chickpea recipe in this section (page 186).

Put all on some pita or flat bread, wrap the end in foil to reduce the mess, and feast.

VEGAN MEAT

Introduction – Vegan Meat

In the grim darkness of the present, vegan meats abound. Seitan, tofu, textured vegetabl
protein, various commercial vegan meats, jackfruit, and tempeh all provide the magical pro
tein chunks to meals. Each of these spread their evil magic in their own way.

Do you need these to "get your protein?" Fuck no! Every goddamn thing has protein. Thes
taste good and provide a satisfaction and familiarity longed for in meals of our non-vega
past.

Seitan, our lord and savior, can be made for mere pocket change. Tofu in the Asian store i
cheap as dirt. Cans of jackfruit mimic shredded meats with perfection. Textured vegetabl
protein makes burger crumble-style substitutes in minutes. Tempeh…just is.

The main concept to consider with most vegan meats is that you must sauté the fuck o
them. Do not char them; that is cause for execution. However, many fail with their seita
especially by not browning it enough and taking the proper time in coaxing the essence o
flavor out of it.

Now, to delve into the vegan meat paradox.

WHERE DO YOU GET YOUR PROTEIN?

The most absurd question that makes every vegan laugh for endless amount
of time: where do you get your protein? Guess what? I am not going to answe
this with a list of foods high in protein. Why? It doesn't matter. I will not cit
various scientific studies showing how much protein you need. Again, it doe
not matter.

Here is the bottom line. If you are getting enough calories, you are gettin
enough protein. Eat a wide variety of vegan foods. Don't just eat a smal
amount of salad each day, and one day you will die…but it will have nothin
to do with veganism. Until that day, you may have a higher chance of feelin
pretty good as opposed to the standard American diet.

At the time of this publishing, I will have been vegan for approximately 1!
years. I take no protein supplements or supplements of any kind. I just fuck
ing eat. It feels like "normal." My normal feels pretty good.

Diabolical tvp Mysticism

SPELL REAGENTS (INGREDIENTS)

TVP

- **TVP** *(textured vegetable protein)*
  (soy based)
- **Vegetable broth**

TVP makes a diabolically more delicious "vegan ground meat crumble" than you would ever imagine. It does not look impressive at first sight. It looks like it will be slightly tasteless, yet this has surprised even gods and monsters.

*The company in this picture does not endorse this book or the Vegan Black Metal Chef project.

1. This is the cryptic spell reagent TVP (Textured Vegetable Protein).

2. Boil some vegetable broth within your tiny cauldron. Invoke a bit less TVP than your vegetable broth.

3. Stir like the mind gone mad. Let it sit for ten minutes off the heat.

Now you are ready to call upon its power in your creations. Do not underestimate this.

TOFU

SPELL REAGENTS (INGREDIENTS)

- **Tofu** *(not silken, but any other degree of firmness)*

Tofu has been declared pariah by the masses through the ages, only coming out of obscurity in the recent past. People still do not know how to prepare this reagent to be the finest offering of the gods.

Insilent Storms in the Tofu Abyss

Though there are many types and levels of firmness, to start out, choose for sacrifice only the "firm" or "extra firm" tofu. I have seen this definition vary in different countries. "Extra firm" tofu here is still a bit soft, like a loose wet sponge or a firm brain. In some countries, it is like a brick you can make a house with. Do not get the brick. It tastes like crap.

The first step in preparing tofu for ritualistic purity is pressing the water out. Do this every time the dark name of tofu is called.

1. Begin by cutting the tofu into triangles, cubes, or whatever fucking shape you want. Form them into the symbol of the ancients upon several paper towels on a plate.

Lay two or three more paper towels atop the symbol of tofu. Place a pot or bowl upon all, and fill it with heavy shit like oil, rice, skulls, or a mace.

Leave this to press the water out for about ten minutes. If this is the first action in any summoning involving tofu, it will be ready by the time you need it.

2. The most common use of tofu in this book will be to deep fry it or pan fry it and add it to a dish. Deep fry just until lightly brown. Too much and it will be as gristle.

STORE-BOUGHT VEGAN MEATS

The swarm of store-bought vegan meats increases year by year. What do I think about them? For the most part, they are fucking awesome! But there is a catch.

To harness their full potential, you must sauté them well in the cooking process. This is the biggest mistake people make when using them. They look pretty good as is without being cooked that much, but then they taste like mild disappointment. This is the principle I have been hammering into your head each and every time when cooking seitan. For example, vegan meatballs look great as is, but you must sauté the outside in some cooking oil for a good bit of time to make them actually taste good and have the right texture. Same goes with various vegan chickun products. Sauté them really well, beyond the directions on the package. After you do this, then apply the concepts you have learned in this book to spice them to the next level.

TOFU WITH CORNSTARCH BATTER

SPELL REAGENTS (INGREDIENTS)

- Tofu
- Cornstarch
- Water

This is the spell to cast a thin, light skin upon the tofu. This ritual is called upon when a slight crunch is wanted upon the tofu without altering its taste much.

In the Shadow of the Cornstarch Batter

1. Of course, following the primary rule of tofu, you shall cut it into strips, triangles, cubes, or whatever the fuck…and press the water out.

2. Pour some cornstarch into a spiked bowl. Grant the cornstarch water to make a fairly thin, watery batter.

   Place the pressed tofu in the muck and let it soak for a few minutes. The tofu will acquire a thin layer of cornstarch upon its outside.

   The purpose of this is not to make a thick batter, but to make a thin layer that does not twist the taste like a knife into your side.

3. Fry like the winds untamed until it is a light golden brown.

Lo! It shall be used in many things.

PANKO-ENCRUSTED TOFU

SPELL REAGENTS (INGREDIENTS)

- **Tofu** *(or anything you want to encrust)*
- **Panko** *(Japanese bread crumbs)*
- **Self-rising flour**
- **Garlic powder** *(optional)*
- **Vegan white wine** *(optional)*
- **Salt**

All tofu begins its life with the fuck squeezed out of it. Pressing the water out of the tofu gives it a firmer, better taste.

Anytime tofu is to be summoned…torture it in this manner first! It will be pressed by the time you need it. It takes about 10+ minutes. Slaughter your vegetables and scald the rice, do whatever diabolical preparation needs to be done.

Thorns of Panko Encrusted Death

1. Cut the tofu into triangles, strips, pentagrams—whatever the hell you want. Place a few paper towels under them on a plate and a few on top. Place a pot or pan upon the tofu over the paper towels, and fill this pot with heavy things.

2. Prepare a summoning bowl with self-rising flour, garlic powder, and salt. The latter spell reagents are optional; if the ritual comes out too salty, neglect them. Fill this with water and a bit of white wine to make a thin batter.

3. Place your pressed tofu in the batter, and coat each piece lightly but well. Materialize some dry panko into another plate, bowl, or pot. Exhume the tofu out of the batter and place upon the panko. Sprinkle more panko over the pieces and coat each piece well. If you are using a pot, you can just shake the pot to coat everything.

4. Plunge the panko-coated pieces into your deep fryer until they are a perfect golden brown. They will look awesome, crispy, and perfect when done.

Your final creation is ready to do your bidding.

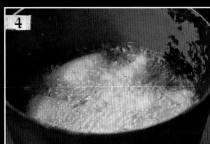

TOFU SCRAMBLE

SPELL REAGENTS (INGREDIENTS)

- **Tofu**
- **Vegan butter or cooking oil**
- **Vegetables** *(spinach, bell pepper, onions, mushrooms, whatever...pick a few)*
- **Spices** *(whatever you want...salt, pepper, sriracha, garlic powder, Italian seasoning, Creole seasoning, etc...seriously, whatever to make a savory dish)*
- **Turmeric** *(for color, optional)*

The magic here is not in the ingredients. The ancient alchemy is the method.

Into Tofu Scramble

Obscurity

The choice of spices matters not. The essence to capture here is the texture. Now, you can be an asshole and pick some ridiculous amalgam of spices…but neither the spices nor vegetables make this dish.

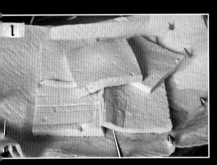

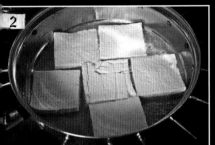

1. The secret to obtain awesome texture lies in cutting the tofu thin. Begin this dark art by cutting the tofu into thin slices. Press the slices between two paper towels like the medieval torture masters of old.

2. Sauté the tofu in a big-ass helping of vegan butter. When the tofu gets slightly browned on both sides, it is time to add the vegetables to this wicked spell.

3. Spice that shit up with your spices. It should already smell somewhat eggy from the browning tofu. Summon forth the salt, pepper, sriracha, garlic powder, a touch of Italian seasoning or whatever the hell you want.

   Add the smallest conjuring of turmeric for color perfection. **Beware!** The turmeric should not be so much that it seriously contributes to the taste. It's not bad, it's just not good.

Scramble like an eviscerating juggernaut. That is fucking it. Serve with toast.

201

BASIC SEITAN

SPELL REAGENTS (INGREDIENTS)

- **Vital wheat gluten**
- **Vegetable broth**
- **Soy sauce or salt**

The primordial vegan meat ritual. While its power, might, and glory are intimidating, summoning it to this realm will eventually be second nature. It takes about an hour, yet requires very little work. Do not call upon our master seitan when you are hungry! This should be prepared well in advance of any meal, and stored throughout the week.

Incipit Seitan

The hardest part about making this is getting off your ass. It's so damn easy, you just have to do it.

1. It starts with a pile of vital wheat gluten. Just pour it the fuck out. However much...just make it happen.

Mix it with some vegetable broth to make a lump of dough. Here is the trick to awesome texture: use only enough vegetable broth to just absorb all of the wheat gluten. It should not be soaking wet. If it is, add more gluten powder. Knead together into a lump and let this sit there while you do the next step.

From here you have a few options of proceeding. The way of least effort and greatest versatility is next. I will go over the other two ways in the online Oracle of Inspiration. Just make this. This is what you are going to want 99% of the time.

2. Fill a pot of water with vegetable broth and a bit of salt or soy sauce. Using a powdered vegetable broth or a bullion cube is far more economical than liquid broth here.

Once boiling, slice your seitan dough into slabs. Drop the slabs into the abyss of nothingness that is your boiling broth.

3. Cover this cauldron, reduce heat to low and simmer. They must undergo this torture for about 45–50 minutes. They will enlarge like a swollen organ as they boil/steam.

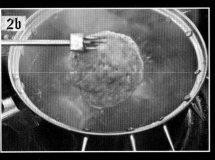

The final seitan brains appear before you! Put in the refrigerator with a bit of the broth. You can use immediately, but cool overnight for even thicker texture.

CHICKUN-STYLE SEITAN

SPELL REAGENTS (INGREDIENTS)

- Wheat gluten
- Tofu
- Vegetable broth
- Soy sauce or salt

Does this vegan meat taste exactly like the pile of putrid flesh that is chicken? No. It has a lighter color, significantly different taste, and cooks in a slightly different manner than the previous *Incipit Seitan*. We shall call this "Chickun-Style Seitan." Fried in breading with a sauce or on a sandwich, you will not give a fuck.

Tormentor of Chickun Souls

The methods of this summoning are the same as the *Incipit Seitan* on the previous pages, with one diabolical twist in the first few steps.

1. Put some tofu and vegetable broth in your blender of oblivion. Liquify into nothingness.

2. Invoke this tofu broth mixture and pour this upon a pile of vital wheat gluten powder. As you mix it, it shall feel extra slimy, weird, and hellish.

   Continue to add wheat gluten powder until it is a non-sticky, oblong pile of dough. It should be neither wet nor bone dry. Get as close to this as possible for ultimate diabolic texture.

3. Slice into slabs and toss into your boiling, salted, vegetable broth cauldron.

   Cover, reduce heat, and simmer in the halls of eternity for about 50 minutes.

The expansion of the seitanic universe shall take place.

CHICKUN NUGGETS

SPELL REAGENTS (INGREDIENTS)

- **Self-rising flour**
- **Chickun-style seitan** *(or regular seitan)*
- **Spices** *(salt, pepper, onion powder, garlic powder, Creole seasoning, any spice blends you want etc.)*
- **Panko**
- **Dipping sauces**

In Nuggets Embrace

1. Spice some self-rising flour in a bowl. It does not even matter what you use. Just add spices that sound good to you with the care of the immortals until that shit looks spiced.

   Leak the crystal blood of water upon it to make a semi-thin batter. Submerge the chickun-style seitan into its depths.

2. Lightly spice some panko using the same spices as the flour. Use a lesser amount than the flour, lest the tastefulness be pushed into the land of harshness and no return.

   Acquire your seitan chickun pieces from the quagmire and cast them into the panko desert. Shake the pot like worlds trembling at their core. This shall coat each piece in perfection.

3. Deep fry the panko-encrusted chickun until Satan is pleased.

Who the fuck does not like fried protein dipped in sauces? You have to be some kind of asshole not to like this shit.

BACONIZING EVERYTHING

SPELL REAGENTS (INGREDIENTS)

- **Liquid smoke**
- **Maple syrup** (*real tastes better than fake*)
- **Soy sauce**
- **Garlic powder**
- **Onion powder**
- **Salt**
- **Pepper**
- **Water**

In the sacred world of vegan culinary alchemy, bacon is more of a verb than a noun. You can baconize damn near everything. Many champions come forth… from seitan, to tofu… or yuba and coconut. Be it mushroom or carrot bacon, all are worthy in their own way.

Just to dispel your mental myths, it does not taste exactly like bacon. What it *does* do is make things have an irresistible, smoky, "meaty" taste. This will approximate everything from bacon to a rotisserie.

This spell will essentially make what the gods call "bacon sauce." You will then apply bacon sauce to various things to make tastes mortals were not meant to experience.

The Bacontine Offering

1. Start out with a blob of liquid smoke. Stare into its black abyss, and remember the quantity of its essence. The amount of other spell reagents rely upon this quantity.

2. This sacred formula requires two times your liquid smoke blob in maple syrup. Splurge and get the real shit. I have tried both, and it tastes better with actual maple syrup. You can get by with the fake crap, but you are selling yourself short.

3. Next comes the soy sauce. The unholy spirit calls you to add a bit more than the initial blob. You will be adding both soy sauce and salt. Deal with it.

4. Sprinkle forth onion powder, garlic powder, salt and pepper. The oracle calls you to speckle it with spices. Smell it! It should smell fucking awesome right now!

5. Finish this ritual by adding almost two times your initial blob worth of water. Just dilute it a bit, lest its strength overpower all of your senses. Also call forth some cooking oil like canola or olive. Add about your initial liquid smoke blob worth of oil.

Now let us apply this sacred liquid in many ways.

CONTINUED

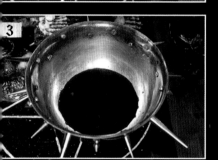

Your final creation is glorious! Look at that shit! Taste it! Fuck!

SEITAN BACON

(or rotisserie chickun, or whatever the fuck it tastes like to you)

1. Cut your seitan into thin-ish slices. You must follow the sacred rule of seitan and sauté both sides until well browned.

2. Pour a thin layer of bacon sauce upon the browned seitan. Yell the battle cry "bacon sauce" as you do this. Stir and boil until the liquid has magically all but disappeared.

YUBA BACON

Yuba is one of the most unseen substances in the universe. It is so unseen, it is not usually even called yuba! You will find this strange being in the frozen section of many Asian stores. Often it is only labeled as "bean curd," so keep a watchful eye. It appears as light, skin-colored sheets or curtains. You can spatter them with blood, hang them around your place of residence, and make the next *Hellraiser* movie.

1. Shred some of the yuba and place in your sacrificial baking pan.

2. Pour a bloody pool of bacon sauce upon it and stir. Heat your hellish oven to 350° F (180°C) and place the pan within.

3. Nay shall you walk away at this critical time. Keep the watchful eye and stir this heap every 6.66 minutes or until it is almost dried and almost crisp. The final creation shall make sandwiches with vegan mayonnaise, sriracha, lettuce and tomato pure decadence.

Follow these same concepts to make tofu bacon, coconut bacon, mushroom bacon, carrot bacon, eggplant bacon…

Whatever the fuck bacon you want.

BBQ JACKFRUIT SANDWICHES

Carving a Jackfruit Giant

SPELL REAGENTS
(INGREDIENTS)

- **Young jackfruit in brine or water**
  (get this at the Asian store)
- **Salt**
- **Water**

VEGAN BBQ SAUCE
- **Cooking oil**

CONTINUED

Jackfruit is a magical, cursed creation. Magical in that it can mimic the taste and texture of many a shredded meat. Cursed in that the terrible, unripe jackfruit taste must be cooked out of it.

Beware the wrong can of jackfruit...use only young green jackfruit in brine or water. Jackfruit in syrup is more like a fruit, not a meat substitute. Also, the brand sadly fucking matters. If there is a more expensive one, and a cheaper one...go with the more expensive brand. I have bought some cheap shit that smelled rotten when I opened it. Personal bias.

Throughout this summoning, you shall encounter several seeds. The seeds are edible, squish like an eyeball, and taste okay. I exhume several of them through the ritual as I see them. If you get a few seeds in the end, fuck it, no big deal. Eat them all if you want.

The downfall of this is that it takes some fucking time. Do not make this when you are hungry and need food now. Each can brings forth about two large sandwiches. It refrigerates well and tastes too good to last long enough to freeze it. You can make several cans if you desire.

◀ 1. This is a can of young green jackfruit in brine. Drain the liquid like the blood of the dead. Boil the innards in a pot of lightly-salted water. Cover, reduce heat to low and simmer like the ancient bubbling springs.

Now the eternal wait begins...

*The company in this picture does not endorse this book or the Vegan Black Metal Chef project.

2. After about an hour of boiling madness, it shall look like Picture 2 and get somewhat soft. At this point, the water may be red like thin old blood. Drain all of the reddish colored water.

Replace with new fresh unholy water and add salt. Cut all of your pieces in half like the splitting of victims on the torture wedge.

Boil once again, cover, reduce heat and simmer like the mind after returning from war.

The jackfruit should look dark with sauce and rich with flavor. Put on an awesome toasted bun.

3. After another 30–45 minutes, drain the newly-formed blood water with skill and valor. Do not lose too many of the jackfruit pieces. Just drain it out of the pot. A colander will let too many of the small shreds go though.

Heat up some oil over a medium flame in a pan or the pot you were using. Sauté the jackfruit and break it up even more. Break that shit up as much as you can, especially the inner cores.

Sauté this for a few minutes.

Now you have come to a fork in your journey. Cease your actions here and remove for jackfruit chickun salad. Keep going for BBQ jackfruit sandwiches (see Oracle of Inspiration on page 217).

Now is the time to replace the flavor of the boiled carcass before you. Acquire a good vegan BBQ sauce and sauté that shit until it "breaks up." Sautéing the sauce removes the vinegary taste. You shall see it separate from itself like the spirit from the body. When this happens, continue.

Rain down water upon your creation, enough to just cover it, and simmer the water away. This will smooth out the BBQ sauce and spread the flavor all throughout the jackfruit pieces.

Taste that shit. Is the flavor diabolically glorious enough? If it still reeks of blandness, add more BBQ sauce and repeat the sauté > water > simmer rite.

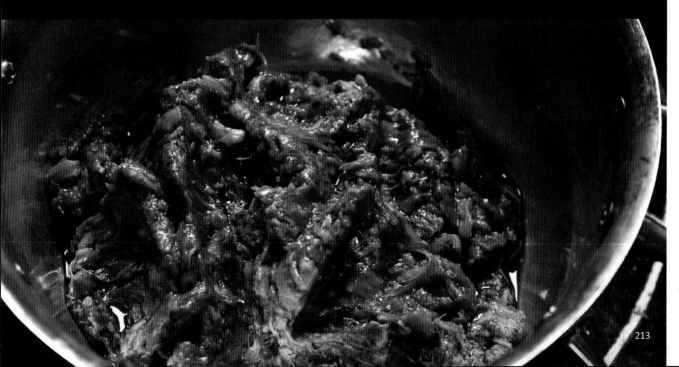

SPELL REAGENTS (INGREDIENTS)

- Tempeh
- Oil for sautéing
- Sauce for smothering or marinating

Cryptic Tempehstorms

Store-bought tempeh is my least favorite of the vegan meats. It has a nuttyish, non-meat flavor that is almost too distinct to be as versatile as the others. However, sauté it well and cover it in enough Buffalo or barbecue sauce, and it is edible.

The gods have decreed that it is also okay if sliced very thinly and marinated or baconized using the sacred baconization ritual on page 208.

This curse does not apply to freshly-made tempeh. If you or a restaurant in your area has access to freshly made tempeh, the game has changed. This can be great, has a more divine texture, and a darkly mild flavor compared with the store-bought tempeh. Order that shit at a restaurant if you see it. Fresh tempeh can awaken your dark senses to pleasing heights.

◀ **1.** This is some tempeh.

2. Sauté it well and smother in Buffalo sauce. Let it marinate in the sauce for a while and put it on a sandwich.

You can make any picture look good. But I will not lie to you. Try everything else in the book first.

The experimentation alchemy shall continue through the ages. You may see more of tempeh in the online expanded Oracle of Inspiration.

Oracle of Inspiration

Vegan Meatball Sandwich

SPELL REAGENTS (INGREDIENTS)

- Vegan meatballs or seitan chunks
- Pasta sauce
- Spices to doctor up the pasta sauce
- Olive oil *(or other cooking oil)*
- Vegetables *(onions, peppers, mushrooms) (optional)*
- Vegan parmesan cheese *(optional)*
- French bread *(or other good bread)*

If you live in the U.S. or several other countries, you can probably find vegan meatballs in many stores. They are becoming popular and easy to find here. If not, use seitan chunks or chickpea bean burger balls. No matter if you are using commercial vegan meatballs or something made from this book, you must fucking sauté the shit out of them. I cannot say this enough. The commercial ones look good and "ready" very quickly. They are not. They will taste like crap. Just like using seitan, sauté the commercial vegan meats really well in your cooking oil. They should not be charred, but take your time in sautéing all parts of the outside. This is critical with all seitan and store-bought vegan meats. Top with vegan parmesean if you have it.

Panko–Encrusted Fried Chickun Sandwich

SPELL REAGENTS (INGREDIENTS)

- Chickun-style seitan *(or any other similar vegan meat)*
- Self-rising flour
- Panko
- Any vegetables you want on a sandwich *(don't forget that avocado exists)*
- Vegan mayonnaise
- Sriracha *(optional)*
- Spices for the chickun breading
- Salt, pepper, garlic powder, any spice blend that are appropriate
- Good bread

Slice a piece of chickun-style seitan semi-thin and follow the methods for the panko-encrusted tofu or chickun nuggets in this section (page 206).

Optionally, toast your bread and prepare each half with a mixture of vegan mayonnaise and sriracha. Of course you can use whatever the hell you want, but this is just a suggestion.

Top with your favorite sandwich shit. Don't forget that bagels make epic buns too.

Scan for updates

Oracle of Inspiration

Jackfruit Chickun Salad

SPELL REAGENTS (INGREDIENTS)

- Young green jackfruit in water or brine *(can from the Asian store)*
- Cooking oil
- Vegan mayonnaise
- White vinegar
- Dill
- Salt
- Pepper
- Onion powder
- Garlic powder
- Mustard or vegan Italian salad dressing *(optional)*
- Sliced green onion or celery
- Good bread *(optional)*

Follow the method of the jackfruit as described in the vegan meat section (page 211).

At the fork in the spell, remove from the pot and let cool for a few minutes while you prepare the dressing.

Mix the ingredients above starting at vegan mayonnaise, using the same concepts as the vegan ranch dressing (page 38). Use only a small amount of either mustard or Italian salad dressing.

Mix with your jackfruit and chill to its depths in your refrigerator.

Eggless Egg Salad

SPELL REAGENTS (INGREDIENTS)

- Tofu
- Vegan butter *(or oil)*
- Vegan mayonnaise
- Vinegar
- Mustard
- Salt
- Pepper
- Onion powder
- Garlic powder

Prepare the tofu with the same methods as the tofu scramble in this section (page 200).

Let cool and set aside as you mix together the ingredients: vegan mayonnaise and below, like the same methods as the vegan ranch dressing in the Euro-American section (page 38).

Add just a small squirt of mustard.

Mix with the tofu, let chill and put on a sandwich or eat by itself.

Index

Credits_____

Author and Photography: **Brian Manowitz**
Layout And Design: **Jenny Ashford**
Vegan Black Metal Chef Traditional Logo Created By: **Maus Corderman**
Vegan Black Metal Chef Extreme Metal Logo Created By: **Christophe Szpajdel**